With this book y...

offer a short course on the basic Christian story to:

- families bringing children for baptism;
- people who have just started coming to church;
- people preparing for adult baptism or confirmation
- church members as a refresher course, e.g during Lent;
- any small group of enquirers.

What this book does

- It uses film clips as a visual introduction to each topic, which makes it accessible to young and old alike.
- It identifies two or three learning outcomes to encourage a mature and sensitive faith.
- It uses two Bible passages to explore each topic, so that the discussion has something of weight to refer to, and that people have something in their hands to reflect on afterwards.
- It uses questions, not ready-made answers, to bring about learning.
- It introduces the participants to a range of different styles of praying which they can use in their everyday lives.

Rev Andy's books: What they say

Bible in Brief
"There has never been a sustained and powerful renewal of Christian faith without a renewed engagement with the Bible. Andy Roland provides a practical introduction to a lifetime relationship with the word of God."
Rt Revd Richard Chartres, former Bishop of London

"This book does what few others do - it offers a very helpful guide for those looking for a brief overview of the Bible and its story."
Rt Revd Graham Tomlin, Bishop of Kensington

"I wish I had read this book fifty years ago. Andy Roland paints with a broad brush, and shows how the different parts of the Bible relate to each other. He tackles difficult subjects with both brevity and clarity. Key passages in Scripture are identified, and helpful questions asked about each to aid reflection. An excellent brief account of the Bible story and its importance today."
Dr James Behrens, barrister

Discovering Psalms as Prayer
"In 'Discovering Psalms as Prayer' Andy Roland weaves together the wisdom of a faithful, personal pilgrimage with practical guidance for reading the psalms. It will be a gift to those wanting to make that discovery for themselves. We are in his debt."
from foreword by Revd David Runcorn,
author of *Spirituality Workbook*,
Choice, Desire and the Will of God etc.

Job for Public Performance
"Like all great works of imagination, Job does not offer us a theoretical solution. It gives voice to the turbulent emotions and declares that the landscape can change. It just is the case that some people learn to live both with questions and with faith, and, as Andy Roland reminds us in his afterword on the book's meaning, this is not an easy place to be; but there is such a place, and Job is one of the greatest guides to its geography."
from the foreword by Rt Revd Rowan Williams, former Archbishop of Canterbury

A Week of Prayer in Jerusalem
"Andy Roland relates his experiences at the grass roots in Jerusalem during last year's 2017 Week of Prayer for Christian Unity. And to those contemplating their first visit to the Holy Land, this book will allow them to soak up some of the atmosphere in advance. Outside of the appendices which are themselves informative and well worth reading, the author has adopted a diary style, peppered with pictures…This is one traveller's tale that is well worth getting hold of."
John Singleton, Methodist Recorder

Five Steps to Faith
"Andy Roland's book is a welcome addition to the resources available for those seeking to understand how and why the Christian Faith matters. It will be widely appreciated."
The Revd Canon Stephen Fielding

"I hope the book spreads far and wide & proves useful to many!"
Rt Revd Graham Tomlin, bishop of Kensington

Look inside all the books at bibleinbrief.org

All about Andy

Although I come from a secure and supportive family, I have always had a fellow-feeling for the outsider. It might be because I went to a boarding school for boys between the ages of 8 and 12. Being small, intelligent, bad at sports and with a Jewish sense of humour was not a good combination. But even back then I was a Christian and I found my faith and prayer a big help.

I studied history at Oxford, and went to St Aldate's Church. On Sunday evenings we ran an open youth club for Oxford's 'unclubbables'. I remember the thrill when after a few weeks I was introduced to the members of a gang. "This is Chopsy, the boss."

On leaving I taught for two years, one in a secondary modern boys' school in Birmingham where I taught R.E. to a class of 13 year olds. In my first lesson I opened by saying, *"Before we start, I want us all to agree on one thing. If the Bible says one thing and science says another, the Bible is wrong. Can we agree on that?"* I knew we had to establish some rules of discourse that they would take seriously. But it took half the lesson for them to accept it. Two weeks later the science master said to me, *"Your boys from 3b have been asking me about the Bible."* "YESSS!" I thought.

In my 30s I worked in Personnel and moved down to London. In the mid-70's revival hit the small church of St Jude's Courtfield Gardens, now St Mellitus Theological College. By a miracle we were able to use a disused pub on the Earls Court Road as an evangelical coffee bar, the One Way Inn, for 1p. per month. We opened from 9pm to 2am four nights a week. The News of the World ran an article on it under the headline, *"The Most Welcoming Pub in the World"*. Some people were converted to Christ, but also, the church was converted to the area. It was a life-changing experience for us all.

After two years at the Post Green Community in Dorset, I read theology at Durham, and did a placement in the prison. (There are almost as many prisoners around Durham as there are university students). As a curate I did an 8 week placement in the Drug Dependency Unit at the Bethlehem and Maudsley Hospital and was introduced to the Twelve Step groups such as Narcotics Anonymous.

From 1994 to 2015 I was vicar of All Saints Hackbridge & Beddington Corner, near Croydon. There I encouraged 12-step groups to hold their weekly meetings in the church and centre. CA (Cocaine Anonymous) I found particularly inspiring and one year they co-led the church's Lent course.

"Five Steps to Faith" arose from a course I developed in the parish for people who were curious about Christianity but were barely even fringe members of the church, typically young couples who wanted their babies christened. Retirement (and a wonderful publisher) has enabled me to produce this book. My hope is that some churches might find it a valuable tool with which to get alongside the curious and uncommitted and help them find that the Christian gospel is both rational and life-giving.

My thanks to

Chris Day of Filament Publishing Ltd: My publisher and mentor. Thank you for making me a writer! And **Zara** for being unfailingly helpful. The website is **filamentpublishing.com**

Daniel Gould drew the cartoons for the text here, and did the fine line illustrations for 'Bible in Brief' and the brilliant map of Jerusalem in 'A Week of Prayer in Jerusalem'.
See **www.dangledart.com**, email: **info@dangledart.com**

Nathaniel Gillet the brilliant designer of all my book covers and of the websites **bibleinbrief.org** and **allsaintschurchhackbridge.org.uk**. His website is **natgillett.co.uk**

Rosie and everyone at St Mellitus College, Courtfield Gardens SW5 for their friendliness and the use of their library for writing and research.

Ruby and all the staff at the National Art Library, Victoria and Albert Museum, for their support and for watching over the most blissful place ever in which to write.

and to everyone at **All Saints Hackbridge and Beddington Corner** who were there at the start of the programme which became "Five Steps'.

The pictures at front page of each section are mostly etchings or sketches by Rembrandt (1606-1669). The first one of God as Creator is an etching by William Blake (1757-1827). The drawing of a bishop confirming a young man is from the Sacred Heart Community, Troy, New York. The drawing of a scroll is taken from Bible in Brief.

FIVE STEPS TO FAITH
+ four follow-ons

How to open up the Good News
to people who don't yet know it

An interactive resource
from
Rev Andy Roland

Published by Filament Publishing Ltd
16, Croydon Road, Waddon, Croydon Surrey CR0 4PA

The right of Andrew Roland to be identified as the author of this work has been asserted by him in accordance with the Designs and Copyright Act 1988

© Andrew Roland 2018 Illustrations by Daniel Gould

Printed by IngramSpark

ISBN 978-1-912635-13-9

The book is protected by international copyright and may not be copied in anyway without the prior written permission of the publishers.

Contents

BEFORE WE START

Introduction	13
The Five Steps Philosophy	17
Getting Ready	21

THE PROGRAMME

Step 1	Who or what is God?	25
Step 2	Who was Jesus?	39
Step 3	The Cross - a tragic mistake?	53
Step 4	Resurrection - can you believe it?	65
Step 5	Holy Spirit - presence and power	77

AFTER SALES SERVICE

Introduction		93
Step 6	Bible ethics: How should we then live?	95
Baptism	Decisions, decisions, decisions: Starting the journey	105
Confirmation	A solution looking for a problem: Embracing the journey	115
Communion	Bread for the journey	127
Keep Calm and Carry on Learning		139

Introduction

THE FIVE STEPS

The Christian world is awash with excellent courses to introduce newcomers to the Christian faith. The most famous is the Alpha Course, but there are also the Y course, Christianity Explored, Pilgrim etc. Why have another one?

'Five Steps to Faith ' is different in 5 ways.

- It is ideal for couples bringing babies for baptism or getting married. Just two couples, plus children, with one or two church members bringing the Five Steps is enough for a great little group.

- It tells the Christian story as a story, using the actual words of the original source material, i.e. the Bible. The five steps are:

God	Creator and Mystery
Jesus	Healer and Teacher
the Cross	Tragedy and Salvation
Resurrection	both Jesus' resurrection and ours.
Holy Spirit	power at Pentecost, and presence in our lives.

The Bible passages are provided as handouts. Each step has two contrasting passages to open up a breadth of understanding.

- It uses cringe-free film clips which introduce the topic and do not try to explain it. They are child and adult-friendly.

- The learning outcomes provide a bridge between how people in our society understand the world and how the Christian story adds a new dimension, without people feeling they have to put their brains into mothballs.

- Each session ends with an appropriate form of prayer, which can be used on a daily basis thereafter.

OTHER FEATURES

- Each step is prefaced with five comments taken at random from members of the general public about the topic, mostly people encountered in the tea rooms of the Victoria and Albert Museum. The reason is to remind ourselves of what people in Britain generally think about the Christian faith, not what we would like them to think.

- Each step has extra resources for the person leading the session, a joke or a story and some basic Bible background. The aim is to make the CCC (Card Carrying Christian) or session leader more confident in responding to questions.

- Each page has wide margins for your own comments and a page at the end of each session for your notes.

AFTER SALES SERVICE

The After Sales Service is made up of four follow-on sessions which can be used according to pastoral needs and opportunities. These are Bible Ethics, Baptism, Confirmation and Holy Communion.

Bible Ethics This is a general session, exploring the Ten Commandments, prophetic insight in Isaiah and New Testament ethics in Paul. It can stand alone, or be an opportunity for the original Five Step group to meet again after an interval.

Baptism This step explores the ministry of John the Baptist and baptism of Jesus, followed by what baptism might mean for us in John 3.1-16.

Confirmation There is more talking in this one, because it goes through the history of confirmation. Discussion is centred round a passage in Acts. A key component is a time of meditation centring on the teaching about the Spirit in John 14.

Communion If someone is being prepared for Confirmation, they need to learn about Communion. This step uses Mark, 1 Corinthians and an extract from the Book of Common Prayer. It could also stand on its own as a separate group session, e.g. on a retreat.

The final step leading to either Baptism or Confirmation or both would be to spend a session going through the actual services as appropriate.

I used the format several times as preparation for baptism or confirmation, always in people's homes, and people did come to faith. It works best on a small, intimate scale. It means that Mum and Dad can take part together without needing to find a babysitter, with maybe another couple also taking part.

My hope is that the specific learning outcomes and the use of open discussion makes it possible for anyone in the church community, any CCC (Card Carrying Christian), to lead it. The sole requisite is that they need to like people.

The Five Steps Philosophy

1. OWNERSHIP

Five Steps should be offered in the home of enquirers. Not in church, not in the vicarage, not in the community centre, not in a churchwarden's home. (I tried it once in a pub and it did not work). This means that both wife and the ("I'm not religious") husband can take part, while the children can watch the film clip at the beginning. And there is no need for a babysitter.

It can also be offered to wedding couples if their interest is sparked off through the preparation for a church wedding.

The hosting couple will naturally offer tea and coffee (one hopes), thereby taking on one aspect of leading the evening. If there is another couple with children, they might take it in turns to host it, so effectively sharing the childcare.

2. STARTING WITH A SHARED EXPERIENCE

The evening starts with a 10-minute film clip, e.g. a clip from "The Miracle Maker". This is an animated film about the life of Jesus, with a grown-up script. It is appreciated by adults and children alike. It means that everyone, the host couple, other visitors, the course leaders, all start off with a common experience.

3. USING THE BIBLE

Each session has a handout with two longish Bible passages printed out. (These can be downloaded from the website bibleinbrief.org to create a double-sided A4 document). Again, the purpose is to provide a common basis for discussion for everyone in the room. The CCC (Card-Carrying Christian) will take the lead, but it is open to anyone to say "But what about this?"

The Bible passage is read aloud by people in the group. Half the passages are set out in a dramatised form, so different people take different parts. The passages have much greater impact if read like this, and even the most agnostic husband will enjoy being God! The other passages should be read round the group; bullet points mark the paragraphs. No one should be pressured into reading aloud; you do not know if anyone may be dyslexic or simply shy. But the act of reading aloud does bolster a sense of ownership.

This way of accessing the Bible can begin to take away the fear of it. If and when they come to a church service, hearing the Bible read will not appear strange.

4. QUESTIONS NOT ANSWERS

My grandfather Thomas Osborne was headmaster of Aylesbury grammar school from 1900 to 1927, and he made it one of the best schools in the country. At his interview in 1900 he was asked what his philosophy of education was. He replied that it derived from the word "education" itself. This comes from the Latin e-ducare, or ex-ducare, which meant to lead out from, not to push into. In other words, learning comes from what we work out for ourselves, rather than what we are told, from discussion rather than lectures.

When I started doing the Five Step course, I used to give a very good little talk on who God was. (At least that's what I thought). Over time, that talk got shorter and shorter, until I simply asked, "What do you think about God?' The replies gave plenty of material for the ensuing discussion. And if you do not try to pre-empt the discussion, you never know what may turn up. I remember asking a family with whom I was talking about baptism what they thought the Holy Spirit was. The dad, who never went to church, replied "the presence and power of God". I have not been able to improve on that since.

5. LEARNING OUTCOMES

Five Steps to Faith is not a purposeless free-for-all. There are specific learning outcomes to each session which are meant to build up a faith which is reasonable and in tune with the central message of the Bible. The learning mode is one of guided exploration. For example, in one Bible study group we had someone who believed that God was physical, that somewhere there was an actual very large body of God, with hands, feet etc. Open discussion had brought out this person's belief, and it was then possible to bring them to a better understanding of "the Love that moves the sun and other stars." (Dante, last line of Paradiso).

6. PRAYER

A step towards faith is useless unless it includes some training in prayer. Prayer is what we do when we want to open our lives more to God. Otherwise everything we do and discuss in relation to the Bible, the Church and even helping those in need, simply stops at the level of head knowledge. So each session ends with a prayer practice, which is rooted in the step of faith we have been exploring and which people can take with them into their daily lives. For instance, after the session on the Cross, the prayer practice is Jesus' own prayer at Gethsemane: "Not my will but yours be done."

Getting ready

It is always an anxious time when you are doing something new. And anxiety rarely has a positive impact on whatever we do. So here are a few tips on how to reduce stress levels if you are about to lead a Five Steps session in someone's home.

Photocopying
Photocopy the handouts and any other material the day before the meeting. If you try to do it an hour before, your printer is sure to run out of ink.

Get acquainted
Read through the session and the handouts. Think through the Learning Outcomes, do they fit with your own understanding? If not, change them for something that does.

Film clip
You will need a copy of 'The Miracle maker' as a DVD or similar media. Have a look at the clip mentioned in the material for the session.

DON'T work out your answers
You could do some background reading if you wish, but don't start to create a small speech which will give people the right answer. That is not how we learn! Let the conversation develop naturally. Use the two questions that are used in the Alpha course discussions: "What do people think?" and "What do people feel?"

Other Resources
Have a look at the "Other Resources" section and see if there is anything you might want to be ready to include. Only use the joke if you think it is funny, and if it fits into the conversation.

The Prayer
Make sure you are comfortable with the Prayer Section. You could practise it with someone beforehand if you feel unsure.

Pray!
Spend some time being quiet with God. And pray for the people you will meet. It can be as simple as *"God, please bless so-and-so and give them what they need."*

Timing
Turn up on time, not more than five minutes' early, because you hosts may be madly dashing round, and not more than five minutes' late because they may start getting anxious that the whole thing is not going to happen. Wear a watch and don't let the session go on longer than an hour and a half. An hour and a quarter is about right.

Step 1
Who or what is God?

WHAT PEOPLE THINK... **about God**

From the Victoria and Albert Museum's Tea Room:

"That's a huge question."

"Still waiting for the evidence."

"The Creator of everything, however you imagine it."

"I think God doesn't exist."

"I don't personally believe in God, but sometimes I'd like to."

FIVE STEPS TO FAITH

WHAT'S THIS STEP ABOUT?

Step 1 starts with dealing with a major misconception in many people's minds about the Bible, specially about Genesis 1, namely you can't believe in the theory of evolution and still be a Christian. You can and you should!

We then explore what we mean by the idea of "God", through God's encounter with Moses in Exodus 3. Don't start with a clear view that you want others to agree to. Give space for a God-shaped question mark to arise.

LEARNING OUTCOMES

1 Evolution and the Bible
The first aim is to prove that the Bible does not contradict the theory of evolution. Genesis 1 is not meant to be a scientific statement, and that can be shown clearly. So when children learn about evolution at Primary School, they don't come to relegate the idea of God to the realm of fairy tales a bit like Father Christmas.

2 The nature of God
The second aim is to show how the being of God is fundamentally mysterious and yet a relationship is possible.

STEP 1: WHO OR WHAT IS GOD?

THE SESSION

FIRST FILM CLIP

I use the start of the BBC film Planet Earth, beginning with a view of the earth from space, leading to the emergence of a polar bear and her two cubs from their winter hibernation, and on to the great caribou migration across northern Canada, ending with the unsuccessful attempt of a caribou calf to escape from a wolf. It shows the beauty of the planet, and the fact that death is always intermingled with life. It takes 12.5 minutes.

If you do not have the DVD, two clips are available on my website bibleinbrief.org of the polar bear clubs and of two young goats escaping from an Arctic fox. These can also be sourced on youtube.

FIRST DISCUSSION

This is simply to get people's reaction from the film. If there are children there, their input is just as valuable as anyone else's.

Note1: You do not need to start by asking people, "What do you think about God?" though that is a possibility. The film clip about the natural world serves to start off the evening.

Note 2: Genesis 1 proclaims that the world God made was "very good". I do not find that easy to say. There is amazing goodness and beauty in the world; but there are also tragedy and human-led deterioration of the planet. If you have difficulties, do not be afraid to say them. I believe that faith grows by facing doubts, not by trying to disown them).

FIRST BIBLE BIT

Genesis 1.1- 2.3
The story of how God made the world in six days.

SECOND DISCUSSION

As a discussion starter you could ask: "Do you think you can take the Bible seriously and also believe in the theory of evolution?

That should create a lively discussion. Hopefully some will say science has all the answers, and others will say the Bible does.

Teaching Point: To prove that the Bible does not intend to tell us about science.

Using the grid on p. 33, you ask people what was created on:

Day 1 Light and Dark
Day 2 Air and Water (In the ancient understanding of the world air being the gap between the upper and lower waters).
Day 3 Land and plants
Day 4 Sun, moon and stars (How do they relate to day 1?)
Day 5 This is the killer! Birds and fishes - they live in the air and water.
Day 6 Animals and humans.

Key question: If this was a stand-alone in a public library, which section should it come under: science, literature, history, poetry, theatre?

What you have is a series of stage sets, which are then populated by actors, e.g. on day 4 the sun, moon and stars come on stage to act in the light and the darkness. It is only scientific in that it gives an organised, ordered view of creation.

STEP 1: WHO OR WHAT IS GOD?

But belief in the orderliness of creation is the foundation of all modern science.

The point of this section is to assure people that they do not have to shut down one part of their brain in order to think about the Christian faith. Don't expect to have all their questions answered - nor yours!

SECOND FILM CLIP

Use two minutes of Moses at the burning bush, in the animated film clip "Moses", from 7'47" to 9'30". You can use the video on the links page of bibleinbrief.org or you can find it on youtube.
(Do watch the whole of this some time. It is a very fine piece of animation, and it won the Outstanding Achievement in Animation award at Primetime Emmy).

SECOND BIBLE BIT

Exodus 3.1-6 or 1-15

Introduce the story so far:

- The Hebrews became state slaves in Egypt;
- Moses (an Egyptian name) was rescued as a baby, and as an adult murdered an Egyptian;
- he took refuge in the desert.

People then read the passage in the dramatised form.

THIRD DISCUSSION

The following question is an important discussion starter. It gives people the opportunity to voice some of their own thoughts about God, but it stays closely linked to the Bible narrative.

Key question: What do you think God meant when he said his name was "I AM"?

Hopefully there will be a confused discussion leading to people saying , "I don't know."

A further question: What would you think if I answered "I am Andy" to every question you could put to me? (This can be tried out in practice in the group, it is quite amusing. At the very least, you would think I was saying "Mind your own business").

There is a useful little book called "The Orthodox Way by Bishop Kallistos Ware. The first chapter is "God as Mystery".

(The second chapter goes on the next obvious thing about God: "God as Trinity")

Key question: How else does God describe himself here?

Hopefully, someone will say, "the God of your father, the God of Abraham, the God of Isaac and the God of Jacob", i.e. someone who enters into a personal relationship with us individually.

Round off the discussion by saying that is as far as we can go at this stage. Hopefully as the weeks progress, there will be more clues about who or what God is.

PRAYER

Explain that every session will end with a form of prayer linked to what we have been finding out about, and which we can use in the week ahead.

This session we take a prayer from the Old Testament. It is the blessing which Aaron, Moses' brother spoke. Here it is turned into a prayer which we can say for ourselves and our families.

> **The Lord bless you/us and keep you/us;**
> **The Lord make his face to shine upon you/us,**
> **and be gracious to you/us;**
> **The Lord lift up his countenance towards you/us,**
> **and give you/us peace.**
> *(from Numbers 6.24-26)*

You can suggest that parents might pray this with their children when they put them to bed; or say it for each other at the end of the day.

FIVE STEPS TO FAITH

OTHER RESOURCES for Step 1

A Joke
A joke is always a good opener. Here is one which fits well in this session.

> A West Indian lady who was a long-standing church member greeted the vicar one Sunday beaming with joy. "You know what, vicar? I had a vision last night and I actually saw God. That's right, I actually saw God! And do you know what, vicar? She's black!"

When were Genesis and Exodus written?
Someone may ask when these books of the Old Testament were written. The answer is no one knows. The earliest manuscripts we have of them are in the Dead Sea Scrolls, c. 0 AD. Most scholars think that the first five books were compiled from various sources and traditions during the exile in Babylon, around the 6th century B.C.

The other creation story
The creation story in Genesis 1 is very familiar. In it the world starts as a watery waste. There is another creation story in chapter 2, when the world starts as a waterless desert.

What about the Trinity?
The Trinity is about the three aspects or dimensions of God, rather than three individual persons, i.e. God beyond us, with us and in us. See my blog, 'God in 3D' at bibleinbrief.org.

STEP 1: WHO OR WHAT IS GOD?

THE SIX DAYS OF CREATION

DAY 1	DAY 4
DAY 2	**DAY 5**
DAY 3	**DAY 6**

FIVE STEPS TO FAITH

STEP 1 HANDOUT

GENESIS 1 (edited)

- In the beginning when God created the heavens and the earth, the earth was a formless void and darkness covered the face of the deep, while a wind from God swept over the face of the waters. Then God said, 'Let there be light'; and there was light. And God saw that the light was good; and God separated the light from the darkness. God called the light Day, and the darkness he called Night. And there was evening and there was morning, the first day.

- And God said, 'Let there be a dome in the midst of the waters, and let it separate the waters from the waters.' So God made the dome and separated the waters that were under the dome from the waters that were above the dome. And it was so. God called the dome Sky. And there was evening and there was morning, the second day.

- And God said, 'Let the waters under the sky be gathered together into one place, and let the dry land appear.' And it was so. God called the dry land Earth, and the waters that were gathered together he called Seas. And God saw that it was good. Then God said, 'Let the earth put forth vegetation: plants yielding seed, and fruit trees of every kind on earth that bear fruit with the seed in it.' And it was so. And God saw that it was good. And there was evening and there was morning, the third day.

- And God said, 'Let there be lights in the dome of the sky to separate the day from the night; and let them be for signs and for seasons and for days and years, and let them be lights in the dome of the sky to give light upon the earth.' And it was so. God made the two great lights—the greater light to rule the day and the lesser light to rule the night—and the stars. God set them in the dome of the sky to give light upon the earth, to rule over the day and over the night, and to separate the light from the darkness. And God saw that it was good. And there was evening and there was morning, the fourth day.

- And God said, 'Let the waters bring forth swarms of living creatures, and let birds fly above the earth across the dome of the sky.' So God created the great sea monsters and every living creature that moves, of every kind, with which the waters swarm, and every winged bird of every kind. And God saw that it was good. God blessed them, saying, 'Be fruitful and multiply and fill the waters in the seas, and let birds multiply on the earth.' And there was evening and there was morning, the fifth day.

- And God said, 'Let the earth bring forth living creatures of every kind: cattle and creeping things and wild animals of the earth of every kind.' And it was so. God made the wild animals of the earth of every kind, and the cattle of every kind, and everything that creeps upon the ground of every kind. And God saw that it was good.

Then God said, 'Let us make humankind in our image, according to our likeness.
So God created humankind in his image,
in the image of God he created them;
male and female he created them.

And it was so. God saw everything that he had made, and indeed, it was very good.
And there was evening and there was morning, the sixth day.

FIVE STEPS TO FAITH

EXODUS 3.1-15 (edited & dramatised)

Narrator. Moses was keeping the flock of his father-in-law Jethro, the priest of Midian; he led his flock beyond the wilderness, and came to Horeb, the mountain of God. There the angel of the Lord appeared to him in a flame of fire out of a bush; he looked, and the bush was blazing, yet it was not consumed. Then Moses said,
Moses. 'I must turn aside and look at this great sight, and see why the bush is not burned up.'
Narrator. When the Lord saw that he had turned aside to see, God called to him out of the bush,
God. 'Moses, Moses!'
Moses. 'Here I am.'
God. 'Come no closer! Remove the sandals from your feet, for the place on which you are standing is holy ground.'... 'I am the God of your father, the God of Abraham, the God of Isaac, and the God of Jacob.'
Narrator. And Moses hid his face, for he was afraid to look at God.
God. 'I have observed the misery of my people who are in Egypt; I have heard their cry on account of their taskmasters. So come, I will send you to Pharaoh to bring my people, the Israelites, out of Egypt.'
Moses. 'Who am I that I should go to Pharaoh, and bring the Israelites out of Egypt?'
God. 'I will be with you; and this shall be the sign for you that it is I who sent you: when you have brought the people out of Egypt, you shall worship God on this mountain.'
Moses. 'If I come to the Israelites and say to them, "The God of your ancestors has sent me to you", and they ask me, "What is his name?" what shall I say to them?'
God. 'I AM WHO I AM.'... 'Thus you shall say to the Israelites, "I AM has sent me to you." ' ... 'Thus you shall say to the Israelites, "The LORD*, the God of your ancestors, the God of Abraham, the God of Isaac, and the God of Jacob, has sent me to you":

* similar to I AM

AN ANCIENT BLESSING (adapted)

The Lord bless you/us and keep you/us;
The Lord make his face to shine upon you/us,
and be gracious to you/us;
The Lord lift up his countenance towards you/us,
and give you/us peace.

(from Numbers 6.24-26)

FIVE STEPS TO FAITH

NOTES

Step 2
Who was Jesus?

WHAT PEOPLE THINK... **about God**

From the Victoria and Albert Museum's Tea Room:

"Oh God! I sometimes wonder who was Jesus, there isn't a historical link to it. I like his main teaching. Some is a bit old-fashioned for the modern age."

"I was raised as a Christian and believed in Jesus, and I wish I had more time now to work out what that means for me."

"Well, I'm slightly an atheist. To me he's a figure of the catholic church which unites the idea of the catholic church together."

"The Son of God, the instigator of Christianity and the moral code as Jesus proposed it, not necessarily as the Christian churches developed it further."

"Maybe a historical figure."

FIVE STEPS TO FAITH

WHAT'S THIS STEP ABOUT?

We look at the recorded ministry of Jesus:
What he actually did two thousand years ago in Palestine.
What he actually said two thousand years ago in Palestine.

LEARNING OUTCOMES

1 The reliability of the gospel
That people come to accept that the gospels give a reliable account of Jesus' ministry, with the gospel of Mark setting the standard.

2 The healing ministry of Jesus
That people come to see Jesus as a real person through particular incidents in his ministry, illustrating his astonishing natural authority in healing and forgiveness.

3 The teachings of Jesus
That people recognise how challenging much of Jesus' teaching is. And that they appreciate the extraordinary authority that Jesus took upon himself.

THE SESSION

FILM CLIP

We watch 9 minutes of "The Miracle Maker", from 17'30" to 26'. This starts with Jesus using Peter's boat to teach the crowd, and goes on to the call of Peter, the start of opposition and the healing of the paralysed man.

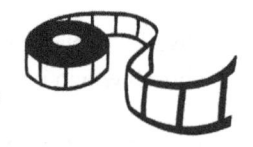

STEP 2: WHO WAS JESUS?

INTRODUCTORY DISCUSSION

Key question: Can we rely on the gospels to tell us about Jesus?

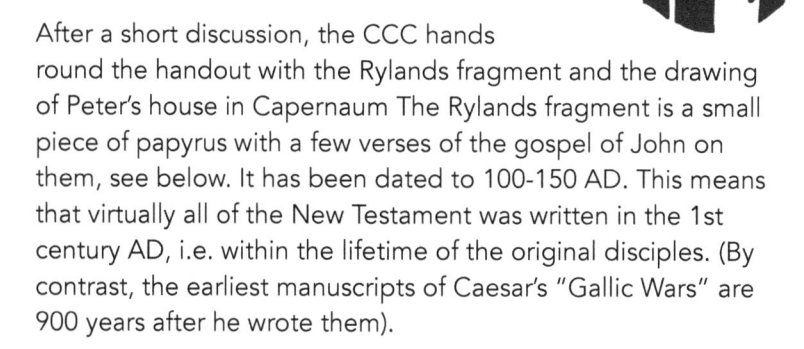

After a short discussion, the CCC hands round the handout with the Rylands fragment and the drawing of Peter's house in Capernaum The Rylands fragment is a small piece of papyrus with a few verses of the gospel of John on them, see below. It has been dated to 100-150 AD. This means that virtually all of the New Testament was written in the 1st century AD, i.e. within the lifetime of the original disciples. (By contrast, the earliest manuscripts of Caesar's "Gallic Wars" are 900 years after he wrote them).

Mark is the earliest gospel because it was used by both Matthew and Luke. Since I believe that Luke was written about 60 AD, this puts Mark at 50 - 55 AD. Also, He includes eyewitness details, like the storm at sea, where only Mark mentions that "other boats were with them." Above all, perhaps Mark was actually there. When the soldiers arrested Jesus in the garden of Gethsemane, *"a young man wearing nothing but a linen garment, was following Jesus. When they seized him, he fled naked, leaving the garment behind."* (Mark 14.51-52) Who was he? He was not one of the twelve. I think it was Mark himself, the writer of the gospel.

FIRST BIBLE BIT

Mark 1.14-18, 29-31, 35, 2.1-12, 2.13-17. The start of Jesus' ministry. The call of the disciples. Healing a paralysed man. The call of Levi. Jesus in bad company.

FIVE STEPS TO FAITH

FIRST DISCUSSION

Ask for people's responses to the passage.

Various points may arise, e.g.
What did Jesus mean by "the kingdom of God"? N.B. It is NOT territory. It is wherever and whenever God is in charge.

What does "Repent" mean? To turn around, get a new mindset. Like switching from Leaver to Remainer, or vice versa. Or changing from supporting Man. City to Man. United, if such a thing were imaginable.

What were fishermen like? Theirs was hard physical work, so they were probably big, burly men, the sort of people you said "Sir" to if you met them in a dark alley.

Jesus prayed early, in the dark. It really was dark, no street lighting. He needed to get away from people to pray and get his marching orders from his Father.

The house where Jesus healed the paralysed man has been excavated, see handout on p. 47.

Key question: What did Jesus NOT do when he healed people?

Answer: He did not pray! He just said, "Get up ". If we acted like that, we would be simply delusional. The problem for the religious leaders was that, when Jesus said it, paralysed men got up!

Second key question: What was the problem with Jesus going around forgiving people?

The problem is best illustrated by acing it out. Ask person A to stamp on Person B's foot, (hopefully not too hard). You then say to person A, I forgive you." What does person B feel about that?

Were the religious leaders right to say, "Who can forgive sins but God alone? (Mark 2.7)

Question: What do you think was the basis of Jesus' authority?
"I don't know" is an OK answer.

SECOND BIBLE BIT

Matthew 5.3-10; 21-24; 38-40; 6.24,25, 33.
Explain that this is part of a collection of Jesus' teaching in Matthew called "the Sermon on the Mount". Ask for people's reactions.

Key question: If I were to say, "The Archbishop of Canterbury says we should all tell people about Jesus, but I say you don't need to bother" what would you think of me?

You would probably say that I was somewhat conceited.
Question: So was Jesus conceited?

Another key question , if time: Are Jesus' teachings do-able? Could be an interesting discussion

PRAYER

I asked five people in the Victoria and Albert Museum's tea room who wrote the Lord's Prayer. None of them had a clue.

Which is interesting, because it actually forms the heart of Jesus' message. It covers all the main bases of his teaching: God as Father, the kingdom of God, living in the present, forgiveness, and help with all the bad stuff there is around.

But it is first and foremost prayer, and we are going to pray it. We use the traditional version, because people are often still familiar with it.

FIVE STEPS TO FAITH

I used to know a canon of Coventry Cathedral. (In the war he had been in the SAS in Yugoslavia and had been captured by the Gestapo not once but twice. He had a slight stammer as a result). He told me that his pattern of prayer was to pray the Lord's Prayer just once a day. But it took him an hour to pray it.

The key is to use each couple of lines as a coat-hanger for our own prayers. This is how we close this session.

The CCC say a line or two, everyone repeats it after him/her, followed by a minute or so silence for their own prayer, like this:

> **Our Father, which art in heaven,
> hallowed be thy name;**
>
> **thy kingdom come;
> thy will be done,
> in earth as it is in heaven.**
>
> **Give us this day our daily bread.**
>
> **And forgive us our trespasses,
> as we forgive them that trespass against us.**
>
> **And lead us not into temptation;
> but deliver us from evil.**
>
> **(For thine is the kingdom the power and glory,
> for ever and ever. Amen.)**

Note: The ending in brackets is probably adapted from 1 Chronicles 29.11, added at an early stage of the Church's history.

A suggestion could be that people aim to spend 5 minutes each day saying the Lord's Prayer slowly and thoughtfully. It is worth having the Lord's Prayer as a small handout for people to keep by them as most people today do not know it.

OTHER RESOURCES for Step 2

A joke

In the film "The Life of Brian", a group of Brian's friends find themselves on the fringe of the crowd listening to Jesus' Sermon on the Mount:
"What's he say? What's he say?"
"Oh, he's just said, Blessed are the cheesemakers. 'Course, he's referring to the dairy trades in general."

How reliable are the gospels?

Mark: The earliest, because it is used by both Matthew and Luke. Has numerous small details which are not in the other gospels because they are not important. e.g. in the storm at sea, Mark tells us that Jesus put his head on a cushoin to sleep. (Mark 4.35-41) After the triumphal entry into Jerusalem, Mark says "Jesus entered Jerusalem and went to the temple. He looked around at everything, but since it was already late, he went out to Bethany with the Twelve. The next day..." Matthew and Luke omit this detail, as they also omit that, after clearing the temple of traders, Jesus also "would not allow anyone to carry merchandise through the temple courts." Mark 11.16.

Luke: Luke is a secondary source, as he says at the beginning of his gospel. *"I decided, after investigating everything carefully ... to write an orderly account..."* (Luke 1.3). We can check his reliability by how he uses Mark, which he does well. For instance, when a young man asked Jesus "Good Teacher, what must I do to inherit eternal life?" Luke faithfully records Jesus' uncomfortable reply, "Why do you call me good? No one is good but God alone." (Mark 10.7,8; Luke 18. 18-19) Luke has his own source for the story of Jesus trial and crucifixion, which varies from Mark's account, e.g. Jesus is sent to Herod, the ruler of Galilee, before being sent back to Pilate.

But above all, only Luke has some of Jesus' most amazing parables: the Good Samaritan, the Prodigal Son, the Pharisee and the Tax-collector.

Matthew: Matthew is my least favourite gospel. He follows Mark quite faithfully and has a lot of Jesus' teachings, much of which he shares with Luke, together with some from his own source. But to me his is a more "churchified" gospel. Often the main person in a parable is changed from a rich Palestinian into a king, representing God, e.g. the Wedding Banquet (Matthew 22.1-11, cf. Luke 14.15-24; and Matthew 25.31-46 where a shepherd becomes Jesus returned as judge. Where Matthew has an incident which is not reported in the other gospels, such as Peter walking on water, and the earthquake at the crucifixion and resurrection, I take it with a pinch o f salt. BUT if we only had Matthew, we would miss the other two, but would not go too far wrong.

John: John's gospel is a completely different kettle of fish. Early on it was called "the spiritual gospel". I find I can make no judgement about it. (A good thing too, I hear you say!) The long conversations and speeches which Jesus makes are unlikely to be precisely reported. On the other hand, all the geographical details are exactly right for Palestine before the destruction of Jerusalem in 70 AD. It is firmly rooted in Jewish society, but is also the most anti-Jewish gospel. Perhaps this reflects the mutual antagonism between church and synagogue at an early date.

All this is all discussed in more detail in the Bible blog at bibleinbrief.org, Can we trust Mark, Can we trust Luke etc.

STEP 2 HANDOUTS

The earliest papyrus fragment, of a gospel. On handwriting evidence, it is generally dated at around 125 AD, the time of the Roman emperor Hadrian, who built Hadrian's Wall. The passages are from John 18.31-33 and 18.35-37. It is on display in the Rylands Library, Manchester.

Archaeologists have found what is likely to have been Peter's house in Capernaum. In the drawing it is the one without a roof.

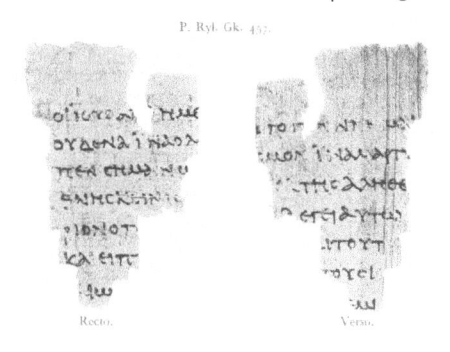

My guess is that Jesus was talking in the open courtyard, which had a light roof of branches and leaves to keep off the sun, and it is this the four friends of the paralysed men broke through.

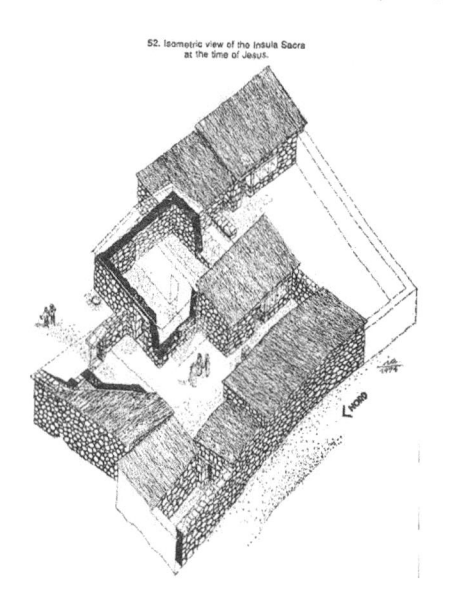

The crowd spread outside the outer gate which is why the four men could not get near Jesus in an orthodox way.

FIVE STEPS TO FAITH

MARK 1.14 - 2.17 (edited)

Narrator Now after John was arrested, Jesus came to Galilee, proclaiming the good news of God, and saying,

Jesus 'The time is fulfilled, and the kingdom of God has come near; repent, and believe in the good news.'

Narrator As Jesus passed along the Sea of Galilee, he saw Simon and his brother Andrew casting a net into the lake - for they were fishermen. And Jesus said to them,

Jesus 'Follow me and I will make you fish for people.'

Narrator Immediately they left their nets and followed him. They entered the house of Simon and Andrew. Now Simon's mother-in-law was in bed with a fever, and they told him about her at once. He came and took her by the hand and lifted her up. Then the fever left her, and she began to serve them.

That evening, at sunset, they brought to him all who were sick or possessed with demons. And the whole city was gathered around the door. And he cured many who were sick with various diseases, and cast out many demons; and he would not permit the demons to speak, because they knew him.

In the morning, while it was still very dark, he got up and went out to a deserted place, and there he prayed.

When he returned to Capernaum after some days, it was reported that he was at home. So many gathered around that there was no longer room for them, not even in front of the door; and he was speaking the word to them. Then some people came, bringing to him a paralysed man, carried by four of them. And when they could not bring him to Jesus because of the crowd, they removed the roof above him; and after having dug through it, they let down the mat on which the paralytic lay. When Jesus saw their faith, he said to the paralysed man,

Jesus 'Son, your sins are forgiven.'

Narrator Now some of the scribes were sitting there, questioning in their hearts, Scribe. 'Why does this fellow speak in this way? It is blasphemy! Who can forgive sins but God alone?' Narrator At once Jesus perceived in his spirit that they were discussing these questions among themselves; and he said to them,

Jesus 'Why do you raise such questions in your hearts? Which is easier, to say to this paralysed man, "Your sins are forgiven", or to say, "Stand up and take your mat and walk"? But so that you may know that the Son of Man has authority on earth to forgive sins' - he said to the paralysed man - 'I say to you, stand up, take your mat and go to your home.'

Narrator And he stood up, and immediately took the mat and went out before all of them; so that they were all amazed and glorified God, saying,

All 'We have never seen anything like this!'

Narrator Jesus went out again beside the lake; the whole crowd gathered around him, and he taught them. As he was walking along, he saw Levi son of Alphaeus sitting at the tax booth, and he said to him,

Jesus 'Follow me.'

Narrator And he got up and followed him. And as he sat at dinner in Levi's house, many tax-collectors and sinners were also sitting with Jesus and his disciples - for there were many who followed him. When the Pharisees saw this, they said to his disciples,

Scribe 'Why does he eat with tax-collectors and sinners?'

Jesus 'Those who are well have no need of a physician, but those who are sick; I have come to call not the righteous but sinners.'

FIVE STEPS TO FAITH

MATTHEW 5, 6 (edited)

- 'Blessed are the poor in spirit, for theirs is the kingdom of heaven.
  'Blessed are those who mourn, for they will be comforted.
  'Blessed are the meek, for they will inherit the earth.
  'Blessed are those who hunger and thirst for righteousness, for they will be filled.
  'Blessed are the merciful, for they will receive mercy.
  'Blessed are the pure in heart, for they will see God.
  'Blessed are the peacemakers, for they will be called children of God.
  'Blessed are those who are persecuted for righteousness' sake, for theirs is the kingdom of heaven.

- 'You have heard that it was said to those of ancient times, "You shall not murder"; and "whoever murders shall be liable to judgement." But I say to you that if you are angry with a brother or sister, you will be liable to judgement; and if you insult a brother or sister, you will be liable to the council; and if you say, "You fool", you will be liable to the hell of fire.

- 'You have heard that it was said, "You shall not commit adultery." But I say to you that everyone who looks at a woman with lust has already committed adultery with her in his heart.

- 'You have heard that it was said, "An eye for an eye and a tooth for a tooth." But I say to you, Do not resist an evildoer. But if anyone strikes you on the right cheek, turn the other also; and if anyone wants to sue you and take your coat, give your cloak as well.

- 'Do not store up for yourselves treasures on earth, where moth and rust consume and where thieves break in and steal; but store up for yourselves treasures in heaven, where neither moth nor rust consumes and where thieves do not break in and steal. For where your treasure is, there your heart will be also.

No one can serve two masters; for a slave will either hate the one and love the other, or be devoted to the one and despise the other. You cannot serve God and wealth. But strive first for the kingdom of God and his righteousness, and all these things will be given to you as well.

- 'So do not worry about tomorrow, for tomorrow will bring worries of its own. Today's trouble is enough for today.

FIVE STEPS TO FAITH

NOTES

Step 3
The Cross - a tragic mistake?

WHAT PEOPLE THINK... **about the crucifixion**

From the Victoria and Albert Museum's Tea Room:

"It's a bit threatening and a bit violent."

"Barbaric."

"I've got very mixed feelings. They adopted essentially an instrument of torture to remember a great person."

"Hope and sacrifice."

"It's not something that crosses my mind."

FIVE STEPS TO FAITH

WHAT'S THIS STEP ABOUT?

The crucifixion of Jesus. What happened and what it might mean.

LEARNING OUTCOMES

1 The story of the crucifixion
To have people take seriously the reality of Jesus' crucifixion.

2 Was there something going in "behind the scenes"?
To wonder if God was in some way directly involved, and if so how and why.

SESSION 3

FILM CLIP

We watch 14 minutes "the Miracle Maker", from 59'30" to 73'. This starts with Jesus in Gethsemane, and we follow his arrest, trials and crucifixion.

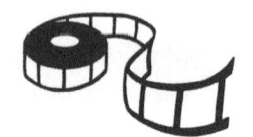

FIRST BIBLE BIT

Mark 15.1-39, edited and read in a dramatised form. People are then asked how they respond to the story.

STEP 3: THE CROSS - A TRAGIC MISTAKE?

FIRST DISCUSSION

Key question: Why do you think Jesus said at the end, "My God, my God, why have you forsaken me?

You might quote what St Paul wrote 20 years later.
'*Christ redeemed us from the curse of the Law by becoming a curse for us, as it is written, "Cursed is everyone who is hung on a tree."*'
(Galatians 3.19, quoting Deuteronomy 21.23)

SECOND READING

The edited version of Isaiah 53 is simply introduced as "A Poem". People take it in turns to read a paragraph. It is very important not to let on that it comes from the Bible.

SECOND DISCUSSION

Key question: Jesus died about 33 AD. When do you think this poem was written?

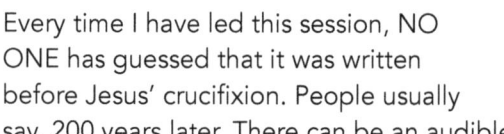

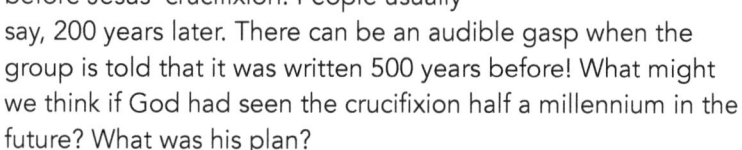

Every time I have led this session, NO ONE has guessed that it was written before Jesus' crucifixion. People usually say, 200 years later. There can be an audible gasp when the group is told that it was written 500 years before! What might we think if God had seen the crucifixion half a millennium in the future? What was his plan?

Key question: What benefits are promised out of this person's suffering?

55

PRAYER

There is a few minutes of silence, during which we repeat inside ourselves the prayer of Jesus at Gethsemane, **"Not my will but yours be done."** We can then take it with us into the course of our everyday life:

To conclude this session, we pray St Richard of Chichester's prayer. One person may pray it; or it can be said with one person praying a line and everyone else repeating that line; or it can be put on a handout so people can read it for themselves and then pray it aloud together.

> **Thanks be to you, O Lord Jesus Christ,**
> **For all the benefits you have won for us,**
> **for all the pains and insults you have borne for us.**
> **O most merciful Redeemer, Friend and Brother,**
> **may we know you more clearly,**
> **love you more dearly,**
> **and follow you more nearly, day by day.**

You could end with everyone saying the blessing from Step 1.

OTHER RESOURCES for Step 3

1 A Quotation
Seneca was a Roman philosopher who lived from 4 BC to 66 AD, so was an exact contemporary of Jesus. He wrote about crucifixion as follows:

"Can anyone be found who would prefer wasting away in pain dying limb by limb, rather than expiring once for all? Can any man be found willing to be fastened to the accursed tree, long sickly, already deformed, swelling with ugly weals on shoulders and chest and drawing the breath of life amid long-drawn-out agony? He would have many excuses for dying even before mounting the cross.

2 Another prophecy
There is a remarkable passage about the shameful death of a righteous man in the book of the Wisdom of Solomon. It is a Jewish book, written in Greek, probably around the time of the birth of Jesus.

> 'Let us lie in wait for the righteous man,
> because he is inconvenient to us
> and opposes our actions...
>
> We are considered by him as something base,
> and he avoids our ways as unclean;
> He calls the last end of the righteous happy
> and boasts that God is his father.
>
> Let us see if his words are true,
> and let us test what will happen at the end of his life...
> Let us test him with insult and torture,
> so that we may find out how gentle he is...
> Let us condemn him to a shameful death,
> for, according to what he says, he will be protected.'

But the souls of the righteous are in the hand of God,
and no torment will ever touch them.
In the eyes of the foolish they seemed to have died,
and their departure was thought to be a disaster,
and their going from us to be their destruction;
but they are at peace.
     Wisdom of Solomon 2.12, 16-17, 19-20, 3.1-3)

STEP 3 HANDOUT

MARK 15 (edited)

Narrator As soon as it was morning, the chief priests held a consultation with the elders and scribes and the whole council. They bound Jesus, led him away, and handed him over to Pilate. Pilate asked him,

Pilate 'Are you the King of the Jews?'

Jesus 'You say so.'

Narrator Then the chief priests accused him of many things. Pilate asked him again,

Pilate 'Have you no answer? See how many charges they bring against you.'

Narrator But Jesus made no further reply, so that Pilate was amazed.
Now at the festival he used to release a prisoner for them, anyone for whom they asked. Now a man called Barabbas was in prison with the rebels who had committed murder during the insurrection. So the crowd came and began to ask Pilate to do for them according to his custom. Then he answered them,

Pilate 'Do you want me to release for you the King of the Jews?'

Narrator But the chief priests stirred up the crowd to have him release Barabbas for them instead.

Pilate 'Then what do you wish me to do with the man you call the King of the Jews?'

All 'Crucify him!'

Pilate 'Why, what evil has he done?'

Narrator But they shouted all the more, 'Crucify him!' So Pilate, wishing to satisfy the crowd, released Barabbas for them; and after flogging Jesus, he handed him over to be crucified.

Then the soldiers led him into the courtyard of the palace (that is, the governor's headquarters); and they called together the whole cohort. And they clothed him in a purple cloak; and after twisting some thorns into a crown, they put it on him. And they began saluting him,

All 'Hail, King of the Jews!'

Narrator They struck his head with a reed, spat upon him, and knelt down in homage to him. After mocking him, they stripped him of the purple cloak and put his own clothes on him. Then they led him out to crucify him.

They compelled a passer-by, who was coming in from the country, to carry his cross; it was Simon of Cyrene, the father of Alexander and Rufus. Then they brought Jesus to the place called Golgotha (which means the place of a skull). And they offered him wine mixed with myrrh; but he did not take it. And they crucified him, and divided his clothes among them, casting lots to decide what each should take.

It was nine o'clock in the morning when they crucified him. The inscription of the charge against him read, 'The King of the Jews.' And with him they crucified two bandits, one on his right and one on his left. Those who passed by derided him, shaking their heads and saying,

All 'Aha! You who would destroy the temple and build it in three days, save yourself, and come down from the cross!'

Narrator In the same way the chief priests, along with the scribes and those who were crucified with him also taunted him. When it was noon, darkness came over the whole land until three in the afternoon. At three o'clock Jesus cried out with a loud voice,

Jesus 'Eloi, Eloi, lema sabachthani?'

Narrator which means, 'My God, my God, why have you forsaken me?' Then Jesus gave a loud cry and breathed his last. And the curtain of the temple was torn in two, from top to bottom. Now when the centurion, who stood facing him, saw that in this way he breathed his last, he said,

Centurion 'Truly this man was God's Son!'

FIVE STEPS TO FAITH

A POEM

- He was despised and rejected by men;
  a man of suffering and acquainted with infirmity;
  and as one from whom men hide their faces
  he was despised, and we held him of no account.

- Surely he has borne our infirmities
  and carried our diseases;
  yet we accounted him stricken,
  struck down by God, and afflicted.

- But he was wounded for our transgressions,
  crushed for our iniquities;
  upon him was the punishment that made us whole,
  and by his bruises we are healed.
  All we like sheep have gone astray;
  we have all turned to our own way,
  and the Lord has laid on him the iniquity of us all.

- He was oppressed, and he was afflicted,
  yet he did not open his mouth;
  like a lamb that is led to the slaughter,
  and like a sheep that before its shearers is silent,
  so he did not open his mouth.
  They made his grave with the wicked
  and his tomb with the rich,
  although he had done no violence,
  and there was no deceit in his mouth.

- Therefore I will allot him a portion with the great,
  and he shall divide the spoil with the strong;
  because he poured out himself to death,
  and was numbered with the transgressors;
  yet he bore the sin of many,
  and made intercession for the transgressors.

NOTES

FIVE STEPS TO FAITH

Step 4
Resurrection - can you believe it?

WHAT PEOPLE THINK... **about the Resurrection**

From the queue trying to get into the Victoria and Albert Museum on Saturday afternoon:

"I don't believe any of it."

"I believe in this because you have to believe in something."

"It's a mystery, isn't it? I believe in it, but I've got no evidence."

"I haven't given it enough thought."

"Well, I believe it, but additionally I would say it is enhanced in the Koran."

FIVE STEPS TO FAITH

WHAT'S THIS STEP ABOUT?

1 Looking at some of the evidence about Jesus' resurrection and weighing its trustworthiness.

2 Thinking about how the resurrection may reveal something of our own future.

LEARNING OUTCOMES

1 Evidence
To accept that there is historical evidence to back up the Church's claim that Jesus rose from the dead a couple of days after dying on the cross.

2 Implications
To think through some of the implications of what we might believe about life after death.

SESSION 4

FILM CLIP

We watch 10 minutes of "the Miracle Maker", from 73' to the end at 83'. This starts with his burial and goes on to his appearances to Mary Magdalene, Peter, the disciples at Emmaus and Thomas, and his final farewell.

FIRST BIBLE BIT

Mark 16.1-8
Note: This is the earliest account, datable, I think, to about 55 AD.

STEP 4: RESURRECTION - CAN YOU BELIEVE IT?

FIRST DISCUSSION

Mark's account breaks off in the middle of a sentence with the word 'for' (in the Greek). Why do you think Mark's account stops where it does?

Key question: Imagine you are a detective, investigating a possible crime scene. What clues are there in these eight verses as to what happened to Jesus?

SECOND BIBLE BIT

1 Corinthians 15.3-8
Note: this can be precisely dated to around 57 AD.

SECOND DISCUSSION

Key question: What events in the film can we link to the list of witnesses Paul produces? Who does he miss out?
Note: He left out the women! Why?

Possible additional reading, Luke 24.1-41 - see separate handout. This can be left for people to read later.

Question leading to the Third Bible Bit.:
BUT if the resurrection is true, what happens to our bodies?

THIRD BIBLE BIT

1 Corinthians 15.35-44a
Note: Again, this was written around 57 AD.

THIRD DISCUSSION

Key question: Paul emphasises both continuity and discontinuity, like the seed and the plant. Does this make sense?

PRAYER

The appropriate form of prayer for the Resurrection is praise and thanksgiving. People might be a little spooked if you suggested joining in a worship song. Here is an alternative:

On Easter Day there is a response which is used by traditional churches which goes back to the earliest days of the Church. I suggest that everyone stands - the natural posture for praise and thanksgiving, and joins in the following response:

CCC	Christ is risen!
All	**He is risen indeed!**
CCC	Christ is risen!
All	**He is risen indeed!**
CCC	Christ is risen!
All	**He is risen indeed!**

While still standing, all say the Lord's Prayer together, including the praise ending:

> **Our Father, which art in heaven,**
> **hallowed be thy name;**
> **thy kingdom come;**
> **thy will be done,**
> **in earth as it is in heaven.**
> **Give us this day our daily bread.**
> **And forgive us our trespasses,**
> **as we forgive them that trespass against us.**
> **And lead us not into temptation;**
> **but deliver us from evil.**
> **For thine is the kingdom the power and glory,**
> **for ever and ever. Amen.**

OTHER RESOURCES for Step 4

1 A Story
A French philosopher during the French Revolution approached Talleyrand, the Foreign Minister and former bishop, to ask his advice on how to create a new religion. Talleyrand replied, "It should be very simple for you to create a substitute for Christianity. All you need to do is have yourself crucified and rise from the dead."

2 Jesus' appearance to Simon Peter
There is an interesting piece of evidence for Jesus' resurrection, which is only alluded to in passing. In 1 Corinthians 15.5, the first person to see Jesus risen was Cephas - the Hebrew name of Peter, who was originally called Simon. In Luke's gospel, the two disciples who see Jesus at Emmaus rush back to Jerusalem and are greeted by the disciples there with the news, "It is true! The Lord has risen and has appeared to Simon!" The film "The Miracle Maker" actually portrays the beginning of Peter's first encounter with his risen Lord.

3 Jesus' appearance to the women
In all four gospels it is the women followers of Jesus who see the angel or angels, and in all the gospels except Mark, whose account breaks off too soon, it is the women who encounter Jesus first. This would not have been invented by the church. Indeed, in Luke's account, "these words seemed to them (the disciples) an idle tale, and they did not believe them." (Luke 24.11) Paul does not mention the women as eyewitnesses, perhaps because the women's testimony would not have been valid under Jewish law.

4 What about the guards?

A powerful episode is the guards set outside the tomb by the Jewish authorities. They experience an earthquake, see the dazzling angel and "lay like dead men." (Matthew 28.2-4) They then go to the chief priests who tell them to start a rumour that the disciples had stolen the body.

It is a dramatic story, but I don't trust Matthew when his account is not supported elsewhere. I think it is a story that got embellished over time. I discuss the trustworthiness of each gospel in blogs on my website bibleinbrief.org.

5 What really happened?

For a brief review of all the evidence, see the blog "What really happened at Easter" on bibleinbrief.org

STEP 4 HANDOUT

Mark 16.1-8

Narrator When the sabbath was over, Mary Magdalene, and Mary the mother of James, and Salome bought spices, so that they might go and anoint him. And very early on the first day of the week, when the sun had risen, they went to the tomb. They had been saying to one another,

Women 'Who will roll away the stone for us from the entrance to the tomb?'

Narrator When they looked up, they saw that the stone, which was very large, had already been rolled back. As they entered the tomb, they saw a young man, dressed in a white robe, sitting on the right side; and they were alarmed. But he said to them,

Young man 'Do not be alarmed; you are looking for Jesus of Nazareth, who was crucified. He has been raised; he is not here. Look, there is the place they laid him. But go, tell his disciples and Peter that he is going ahead of you to Galilee; there you will see him, just as he told you.'

Narrator So they went out and fled from the tomb, for terror and amazement had seized them; and they said nothing to anyone, for they were afraid...

1 Corinthians 15.3-8

- For I handed on to you as of first importance what I in turn had received: that Christ died for our sins in accordance with the scriptures, and that he was buried, and that he was raised on the third day in accordance with the scriptures, and that he appeared to Cephas (Peter), then to the twelve. Then he appeared to more than five hundred brothers and sisters at one time, most of whom are still alive, though some have died. Then he appeared to James, then to all the apostles. Last of all, as to someone untimely born, he appeared also to me.

1 Corinthians 15.35-44 (edited)

- But someone will ask, 'How are the dead raised? With what kind of body do they come?'

- Fool! What you sow does not come to life unless it dies. And as for what you sow, you do not sow the body that is to be, but a bare seed, perhaps of wheat or of some other grain. But God gives it a body as he has chosen, and to each kind of seed its own body. Not all flesh is alike, but there is one flesh for human beings, another for animals, another for birds, and another for fish. There is one glory of the sun, and another glory of the moon, and another glory of the stars; indeed, star differs from star in glory.

- So it is with the resurrection of the dead. What is sown is perishable, what is raised is imperishable. It is sown in dishonour, it is raised in glory. It is sown in weakness, it is raised in power. It is sown a physical body, it is raised a spiritual body.

FIVE STEPS TO FAITH

Luke 24.13-43 (edited)

- Now that same day two of them were going to a village called Emmaus, about seven miles from Jerusalem, and talking with each other about all these things that had happened. While they were talking and discussing, Jesus himself came near and went with them, but their eyes were kept from recognising him. And he said to them, 'What are you discussing with each other while you walk along?' They stood still, looking sad. Then one of them, called Cleopas, answered him, 'Are you the only stranger in Jerusalem who does not know the things that have taken place there in these days?' He asked them, 'What things?' They replied, 'The things about Jesus of Nazareth, who was a prophet mighty in deed and word before God and all the people, and how our chief priests and leaders handed him over to be condemned to death and crucified him. But we had hoped that he was the one to redeem Israel. Yes, and besides all this, it is now the third day since these things took place. Moreover, some women of our group astounded us. They were at the tomb early this morning, and when they did not find his body there, they came back and told us that they had indeed seen a vision of angels who said that he was alive. Some of those who were with us went to the tomb and found it just as the women had said; but they did not see him.'

- Then he said to them, 'Oh, how foolish you are, and how slow of heart to believe all that the prophets have declared! Was it not necessary that the Messiah should suffer these things and then enter into his glory?' Then beginning with Moses and all the prophets, he interpreted to them the things about himself in all the scriptures.

- As they came near the village to which they were going, he walked ahead as if he were going on. But they urged him strongly, saying, 'Stay with us, because it is almost evening and the day is now nearly over.' So he went in to stay with them. When he was at the table with them, he took bread, blessed and broke it, and gave it to them. Then their eyes were opened, and they recognised him; and he vanished from their sight.

- They said to each other, 'Were not our hearts burning within us while he was talking to us on the road, while he was opening the scriptures to us?' That same hour they got up and returned to Jerusalem; and they found the eleven and their companions gathered together. They were saying, 'The Lord has risen indeed, and he has appeared to Simon!' Then they told what had happened on the road, and how he had been made known to them in the breaking of the bread.

- While they were talking about this, Jesus himself stood among them and said to them, 'Peace be with you.' They were startled and terrified, and thought that they were seeing a ghost. He said to them, 'Why are you frightened, and why do doubts arise in your hearts? Look at my hands and my feet; see that it is I myself. Touch me and see; for a ghost does not have flesh and bones as you see that I have.' And when he had said this, he showed them his hands and his feet. While in their joy they were disbelieving and still wondering, he said to them, 'Have you anything here to eat?' They gave him a piece of broiled fish, and he took it and ate in their presence.

NOTES

Step 5
Holy Spirit - Presence and Power

"When the Holy Spirit comes you shall be my witnesses"

WHAT PEOPLE THINK... about the Holy Spirit

From the Victoria and Albert Museum Tea Rooms:

"I think very little about the Holy Spirit. I'm an atheist."

"It doesn't figure in my thinking, because I believe in God as a whole."

"I believe it exists and sometimes I feel it. I'm Catholic, and I think the angels, the guardian angels protect me from harm."

"I don't know. I'm not a religious person."

"The Holy Spirit is not part of everyday life, most people are occupied in their own busyness. In times of trouble or in times of grief, the Holy Spirit becomes a larger presence in people's lives."

FIVE STEPS TO FAITH

WHAT'S THIS STEP ABOUT?

1 The supernatural power that Jesus disciples experienced on the day of Pentecost and its outcome in growing the church.

2 The Holy Spirit as a day to day resource for all Christians. Romans 8 as a design for our lives.

3 Using silence/listening as prayer.

LEARNING OUTCOMES

1 Pentecost
To hear the whole story of Pentecost: the supernatural experience; preaching to the crowd; 5,000 baptised; the life of the first believers. (Acts 2.1-42)

2 Presence of the Spirit in our lives
To understand the daily choice we have of living according to the Spirit or living according to the Ego. (Romans 8,1-17)

3 Prayer
To practice listening to the Spirit as an inner voice; to find that silence can allow us to hear God's word to us.

THE SESSION

FILM CLIP

"Holy Spirit" by the Bible Project. It lasts 4 minutes. Available on bibleinbrief.org and on youtube.

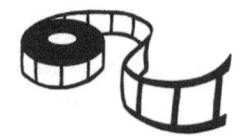

STEP 5: HOLY SPIRIT

FIRST BIBLE BIT

Acts 2.1-42, edited

FIRST DISCUSSION

Introduce this section by saying what Peter did not expect to happen when he had his breakfast cornflakes that morning. He did not expect:

- to receive a powerful spiritual experience which got them all speaking in new languages;
- to go outside the house with his fellow disciples and make a public exhibition of themselves praising God;
- to attract a large multinational crowd;
- to be pushed to the front to make a speech as the spokesman;
- to have many (3,000!) in the crowd react by asking, "What should we do?"
- At that point I believe he had an inspiration or nudge from the Holy Spirit to deal with this new situation. While going around with Jesus, they had baptised no one, expect perhaps at the beginning of Jesus' ministry. Now he thought back to his early days following John the Baptist, and said: *"Repent, and be baptised every one of you in the name of Jesus Christ, so that your sins may be forgiven, and you will receive the Holy Spirit."* (Acts 2.38)

Key question: What would you think if you had been in that Pentecost crowd?

FIVE STEPS TO FAITH

SECOND BIBLE BIT

Romans 8.1-17 (edited)
Here we move from the historical to the personal. Paul's chapter 8 in Romans is perhaps the best summary there is of the Christian life. But he uses words which are easily misunderstood. So there are two handouts. In the first the text translates certain words into modern terms, e.g.

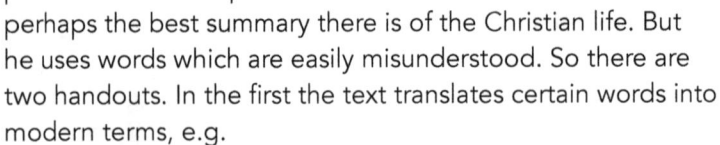

    sin = self-centredness
    flesh = the ego
    law = religion, or general principle like the law of gravity.
    in Christ = inhabiting Christ etc.
    righteousness = both righteousness and justice; the core meaning is being upright, morally and legally.
    spirit = God's spirit and ours, Here, unlike in standard Bibles, I always spell it with a small 's', as there were no lower case letters in books when the New Testament was written. All letters were written as capitals with no punctuation and no spaces between words. Lower case letters for books were only developed in the 9th century. So there may be ambiguity in which a reference could be either to God's spirit or to ours. Perhaps that ambiguity was deliberate.
    body = the physical nature. it has no negative meaning. In v 13 I translate it as 'physical world'.

The NRSV translation is also provided as a check.

SECOND DISCUSSION

Key question: Does any of this chime in with your own experience?

PRAYER & MEDITATION

INTRODUCTION

Explain that we are going to try an experiment, what it is like to pray in silence, without words. St Paul certainly knew it. In Romans 8.26-27 he said:

Likewise the Spirit helps us in our weakness; for we do not know how to pray as we ought, but that very Spirit intercedes with sighs too deep for words. And God, who searches the heart, knows what is the mind of the Spirit, because the Spirit intercedes for the saints according to the will of God.

Praying in the Sprit means moving beyond words, perhaps praying in tongues; most commonly using the prayer of silence, sometimes called meditation or contemplation, or simply being still, seeking God's guidance.

a) Contemplation/meditation

St John of the Cross, a Spanish Carmelite friar of the 16th Century condensed all he knew about contemplation into a four-line poem, 'Summary of Perfection':

> *Forgetting what is created,*
> *Remembering the Creator,*
> *Focussing on what is within,*
> *And stay there, loving the Beloved.*

Here we aim to enter a stillness with God and allow him to refresh us at a deep level, using a "focus word" to keep turning our thoughts back to stillness. The anonymous writer of the 14th century book of direction, "The Cloud of Unknowing", said,

"Lift up your heart to God with a gentle stirring of love; and mean Himself and none of his gifts... Do not stop, but work on it. For at the first time you do it, you will find only a darkness, and as it were a cloud of unknowing, of what you know not, except what you feel in your will as a naked intent towards God... "

Our part is to sit comfortably but alert, and not pay attention to passing thoughts. We will get lots of thoughts. We simply pay them no attention but use a "focus word" to keep coming back to interior stillness. The focus word should be a short one which we find helpful in directing our attention to God.

In the Centring Prayer movement the normal recommended time is 20 minutes twice a day, but that is quite an ask.

b) Guidance

The other type of silent prayer is prayer for guidance. This is particularly practised by members of Alcoholics Anonymous and similar 12 step groups.

"On awakening let us think about the twenty-four hours ahead. We consider our plans for the day. Before we begin, we ask God to direct our thinking, especially asking that it be divorced from self-pity, dishonest or self-seeking motives… We may face indecision… Here we ask God for inspiration, an intuitive thought or a decision. We relax and take it easy… What used to be the hunch or the occasional inspiration gradually becomes a working part of the mind…" (Alcoholics Anonymous, p.86)

In that stillness we may receive a thought which has a kind of weight. It is important to write down the thoughts that come to us. Early AA stressed the need to write things down, and follow up with action. When John Wimber, founder of the Vineyard churches, was asked what is it like to hear the Holy Spirit, he simply said, "You get a hunch."

PRAYER

DOING IT

Provide a pen/pencil and paper for anyone who wants to write down any particular thoughts that come to them.

Ask someone to be the timekeeper, and say how long the silence will last. it could be 10 minutes, 5 minutes or 2 minutes.

End the silence by saying together the Lord's Prayer.

After the Lord's Prayer let anyone who wishes share the thought they had. Nothing, or I'd rather not, are OK responses.

End with saying together the Grace:

> **May the grace of our Lord Jesus Christ,**
> **and the love of God,**
> **and the fellowship of the Holy Spirit**
> **be with us now and evermore. Amen.**

OTHER RESOURCES for Step 5

A joke
The pastor was greeting folks at the door after the service. A woman said, "Pastor, that was a very good sermon." The pastor said, "Oh, I have to give the credit to the Holy Spirit." The woman replied, "It wasn't THAT good!"

What's in a word?
"Holy Spirit" is often mentioned in the Bible, church services and hymns. Another expression found in old-fashioned Bibles and hymns is 'Holy Ghost'. Both phrases mean exactly the same. "Ghost" is the old Germanic word for spirit. Indeed, the word for "spirit" in modern German is "Geist".

In Hebrew the word we translate as "spirit" is 'ruach' (pronounced like a Scottish loch). It also means breath or wind. The New Testament was written in Greek and the Greek word for 'spirit' is 'pneuma'. which also means 'breath"or 'wind'. It is where we get the term 'pneumatic tyre'. The classic example is John 3.8 where Jesus deliberately uses a pun: *"The wind blows where it chooses, and you hear the sound of it, but you do not know where it comes from or where it goes. So it is with everyone who is born of the Spirit."*

What now?
After the last four sessions, we might be asking, "What's next?" That is exactly the question that the disciples asked Jesus after his resurrection. This was his reply:
"You will receive power when the Holy Spirit has come upon you; and you will be my witnesses in Jerusalem, in all Judaea and Samaria, and to the ends of the earth." (Acts 1.8)

Pentecost
Pentecost means 50, because it comes 49 (or 50) days after Passover. The Jewish title is the Feast of Weeks, i.e. seven weeks/49 days after Passover. It was one of the three great pilgrim feasts for Jews, also called the Feast of Harvest and the Feast of First Fruits. In modern Judaism it particularly celebrates the giving of the Law at Mount Sinai.

Christ?

On the day of the Pentecost, Peter announced, *"Let the entire house of israel know with certainty that God has made him both Lord and Christ this Jesus whom you crucified."* But what does the title 'Christ' mean? It is simply the Greek translation of the Hebrew *Mashiach* or *Messiah*. Which means *anointed* or *the Anointed One*.

You could ask who in England has been anointed. The answer (apart from bishops) is the queen at her coronation. Two people were anointed in ancient Israel, the king and the high priest. In Jesus' time the Essenes, a radical Jewish sect, looked forward to the coming of '*the Messiah of David and the Messiah or Aaron*' i.e. the future priest-king to lead Israel. Peter is claiming that person is Jesus.

Psalm 133.2 describes the proces of anointing.
It is like the precious oil on the head,
running down upon the beard,
on the beard of Aaron,
running down over the collars of his robes.
You can offer to anoint a member of the group. You then ask for a bottle of olive oil and threaten to pour the whole lot over his/her head. They will remember it!

Gifts of the Spirit

Some parts of the Church talk a lot about "spiritual gifts", meaning supernatural gifts often used in worship. It is used in 1 Corinthians 12.1, at the start of Paul's list of various spiritual gifts. Paul always refers to these as the work of the Spirit, e.g. *"There are different kinds of gifts but the same Spirit."* (1 Corinthians 12.4)

The gifts which Paul lists in 1 Corinthians 12.7-11 are: wisdom, knowledge, faith, healing, miracles, prophecy, discerning of spirits, tongues and interpretation of tongues. Praying in tongues is particularly important in Pentecostal churches, though it is also known in other churches. However, the point that Paul is making is not that they are terribly important, but that the most important thing is unity and love. *"If I speak in the tongues of mortals and of angels, but do not have love, I am a noisy gong or a clanging cymbal."* (1 Corinthians 13,1)

In Romans 12.4-8 he has another list: prophesying, serving, teaching, encouraging, giving, leading, doing acts of mercy.
In Ephesians 4.11 the gifts of grace are people: apostles, evangelists, pastor and teachers.

FIVE STEPS TO FAITH

> **STEP 5 HANDOUT**

Acts of the Apostles 2.1-42 (edited)

Narrator. When the day of Pentecost had come, they were all together in one place. And suddenly from heaven there came a sound like the rush of a violent wind, and it filled the entire house where they were sitting. Divided tongues, as of fire, appeared among them, and a tongue rested on each of them. All of them were filled with the Holy Spirit and began to speak in other languages, as the Spirit gave them ability.

Now there were devout Jews from every nation under heaven living in Jerusalem. And at this sound the crowd gathered and was bewildered, because each one heard them speaking in their native language. Astonished, they asked,
Crowd 1 'Are not all these who are speaking Galileans? And how is it that we hear, each of us, in our own native language? Parthians, Medes, Elamites, etc. - in our own languages we hear them speaking about God's deeds of power.'
Narrator All were amazed and perplexed, saying to one another,
Crowd 1 'What does this mean?'
Narrator Others sneered and said, '
Crowd 2 They are filled with new wine.'
Narrator But Peter, standing with the eleven, raised his voice and addressed them:
Peter 'Men of Judea and all who live in Jerusalem, let this be known to you, and listen to what I say. Indeed, these are not drunk, as you suppose, for it is only nine o'clock in the morning. No, this is what was spoken through the prophet Joel:

> "In the last days it will be, God declares,
> that I will pour out my Spirit upon all flesh,
> and your sons and your daughters shall prophesy,
> and your young men shall see visions,
> and your old men shall dream dreams...
> Then everyone who calls on the name of the Lord shall be saved."

'You that are Israelites, listen to what I have to say: Jesus of Nazareth, a man attested to you by God with deeds of power, wonders, and signs that God did through him among you, as you yourselves know - this man, handed over to you according to the definite plan and foreknowledge of God, you crucified and killed by the hands of those outside the law. But God raised him up, having freed him from death, because it was impossible for him to be held in its power.

'Fellow Israelites, I may say to you confidently of our ancestor David that he both died and was buried, and his tomb is with us to this day. Since he was a prophet, he knew that God had sworn with an oath to him that he would put one of his descendants on his throne. Foreseeing this, David spoke of the resurrection of the Messiah, saying,
 "He was not abandoned to Hades,
  nor did his flesh experience corruption."
This Jesus God raised up, and of that all of us are witnesses. Being therefore exalted at the right hand of God, and having received from the Father the promise of the Holy Spirit, he has poured out this that you both see and hear… Therefore let the entire house of Israel know with certainty that God has made him both Lord and Messiah this Jesus whom you crucified.'

Narrator Now when they heard this, they were cut to the heart and said to Peter and to the other apostles,
Crowd 'Brothers, what should we do?'
Peter 'Repent, and be baptized every one of you in the name of Jesus Christ so that your sins may be forgiven; and you will receive the gift of the Holy Spirit. For the promise is for you, for your children, and for all who are far away, everyone whom the Lord our God calls to him.'
Narrator So those who welcomed his message were baptized, and that day about three thousand persons were added. They devoted themselves to the apostles' teaching and fellowship, to the breaking of bread and the prayers.

Romans 8.1-17 (edited)
(interpreted text)

- There is therefore now no condemnation for those who inhabit Christ Jesus. For the principle of the spirit of life in Christ Jesus has set you free from the principle of self and of death. For God has done what religion, weakened by the ego, could not do: by sending his own son in the likeness of the self-centred ego, and to deal with self-centredness, he condemned self-centredness from within the human ego, so that the proper requirement of religion might be fulfilled in us, who walk not according to the ego but according to the spirit.

- For those who live according to the ego have the mindset of the ego, but those who live spiritually have the mindset of the spirit. To have the mindset of the ego is death, but to have the spiritual mindset is life and peace. For this reason the mindset of the ego is hostile to God; it does not submit to God's religion - indeed it cannot, and those who inhabit the ego cannot please God.

- But you do not inhabit the ego; you inhabit the spirit, since God's spirit inhabits you. Anyone who does not have the spirit of Christ does not belong to him. But if Christ inhabits you, though the body is dead because of self-centredness, the spirit is life because of having been set upright. If the spirit of him who raised Jesus from the dead inhabits you, he who raised Christ from the dead will give life to your mortal bodies also through his spirit that dwells in you.

- So then, brothers and sisters, we are debtors, not to the ego, to live according to the ego - for if you live according to the ego, you will die; but if by the spirit you put to death the deeds of the body, you will live. For all who are led by God's spirit are children of God. For you did not receive a spirit of slavery to fall back into fear, but you have received a spirit of adoption. When we cry, 'Abba! Father!' it is that very spirit bearing witness with our spirit that we are children of God, and if children, then heirs, heirs of God and joint heirs with Christ - if, in fact, we suffer with him so that we may also be glorified with him.

Romans 8.1-17 (edited)
(actual text - New Revised Standard Version)

- There is therefore now no condemnation for those who are in Christ Jesus. For the law of the Spirit of life in Christ Jesus has set you free from the law of sin and of death. For God has done what the law, weakened by the flesh, could not do: by sending his own Son in the likeness of sinful flesh, and to deal with sin, he condemned sin in the flesh, so that the just requirement of the law might be fulfilled in us, who walk not according to the flesh but according to the Spirit.

- For those who live according to the flesh set their minds on the things of the flesh, but those who live according to the Spirit set their minds on the things of the Spirit. To set the mind on the flesh is death, but to set the mind on the Spirit is life and peace. For this reason the mind that is set on the flesh is hostile to God; it does not submit to God's law - indeed it cannot, and those who are in the flesh cannot please God.

- But you are not in the flesh; you are in the Spirit, since the Spirit of God dwells in you. Anyone who does not have the Spirit of Christ does not belong to him. But if Christ is in you, though the body is dead because of sin, the Spirit is life because of righteousness. If the Spirit of him who raised Jesus from the dead dwells in you, he who raised Christ from the dead will give life to your mortal bodies also through his Spirit that dwells in you.

- So then, brothers and sisters, we are debtors, not to the flesh, to live according to the flesh - for if you live according to the flesh, you will die; but if by the Spirit you put to death the deeds of the body, you will live. For all who are led by the Spirit of God are children of God. For you did not receive a spirit of slavery to fall back into fear, but you have received a spirit of adoption. When we cry, 'Abba! Father!' it is that very Spirit bearing witness with our spirit that we are children of God, and if children, then heirs, heirs of God and joint heirs with Christ - if, in fact, we suffer with him so that we may also be glorified with him.

Romans 8.26-27

Likewise the Spirit helps us in our weakness; for we do not know how to pray as we ought, but that very Spirit intercedes with sighs too deep for words. And God, who searches the heart, knows what is the mind of the Spirit, because the Spirit intercedes for the saints according to the will of God.

NOTES

FIVE STEPS TO FAITH

After Sales Service

INTRODUCTION

Once people have taken part in the Five Steps, what then?

Well, they could simply start coming to church on Sundays and join the local church community.

They could take a break and then come back together for a follow-on step about Bible Ethics, 'How should we then live?'

They could start reading the Bible for themselves on a regular basis using one of the many Bible aids. One option is 'Bible in Brief', which you can find on Amazon or bibleinbrief.org.

They could focus on bringing their children to baptism, and do the step for this.

They could focus on making a personal commitment themselves in confirmation, if not now then perhaps later.

They could have a session thinking about Holy Communion.

They could use 'Five Steps to Faith' with another family or friends.

They could take another course, like Alpha or Pilgrim, to deepen their knowledge and experience of the faith.

Whatever happens, I hope that "Five Steps to Faith" is the start of a spiritual journey, not the end of it.

FIVE STEPS TO FAITH

Step 6
Bible Ethics - how should we then live?

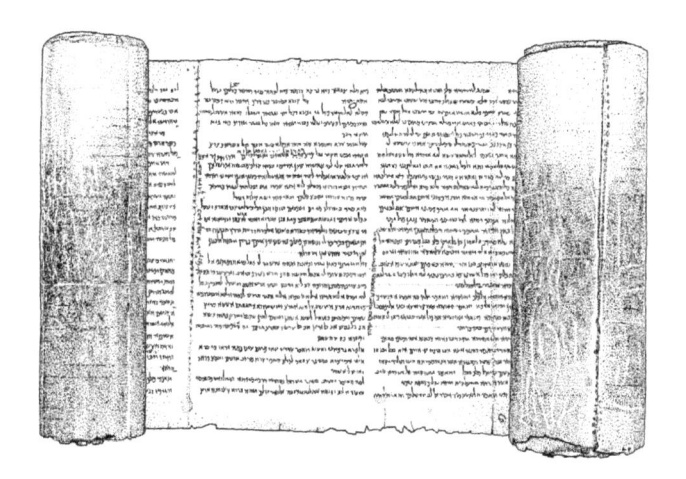

WHAT PEOPLE THINK... about Bible Ethics

especially about the The Commandments

From the Victoria and Albert Museum Tea Rooms:

"Out of date."

"Good in principle, a good thing for society to follow."

"Disjointed with modern society."

"Open to a bit of interpretation but good guidance."

"I'm not religious, so I do not have any opinion of them."

FIVE STEPS TO FAITH

WHAT'S THIS STEP ABOUT?

This step explores what the Bible says about how we should live. We start at the Ten Commandments, then look at what the prophet Isaiah had to say about religion without a social conscience, and end with St Paul's summary of the Christian lifestyle.

LEARNING OUTCOMES?

1 The Ten Commandments
To think about the Ten Commandments, and their relevance to life today.

2 Religion: good or bad?
To realise that religion is a two-edged sword: it can lead people to doing God's will, or it can reinforce our own ego.

3 Christian lifestyle
To grasp something of the challenge of the Christian lifestyle.

THE SESSION

Bible Ethics

FILM CLIP

There is a wonderful film comedy based on an early novel of Jane Austen called "Love and Friendship". Half way through there is a very funny section in which Sir James Martin, not the sharpest tool in the box, talks about the 'Twelve Commandments'. On DVD it is the first two minutes of scene 6. A great introduction to this step if you have the film. And it is worth getting anyway.

STEP 6: BIBLE ETHICS - HOW SHOULD WE THEN LIVE?

FIRST BIBLE BIT

Exodus 20.1-17, heavily edited!

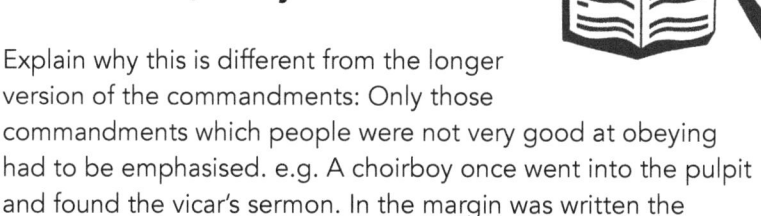

Explain why this is different from the longer version of the commandments: Only those commandments which people were not very good at obeying had to be emphasised. e.g. A choirboy once went into the pulpit and found the vicar's sermon. In the margin was written the comment: *"Weak point here. Shout louder."*

FIRST DISCUSSION

Key question: If you were only allowed Eight Commandments, which two would you drop?

This allows people to think through what commandments we take as read, and what commandments we find hard to take seriously. From God's point of view, what it the purpose of the commandments?

SECOND BIBLE BIT

Isaiah 1.10-17, edited
Explanation: Probably written about 620-600 BC, after Israel, the northern kingdom, had been swallowed up by the Assyrian empire. Only Judah and Jerusalem were left.

SECOND DISCUSSION

Key question 1: How did the people celebrate their religion?
Key question 2: What does God want them to make their priority instead? How does this translate into our society?

FIVE STEPS TO FAITH

THIRD BIBLE BIT

Romans 12.9-18, 21; 13.8-10

THIRD DISCUSSION

Key question 1: "Overcome evil with good". What examples do you know of this?
Key question 2: What is love?

PRAYER

In this session we practice an easy form of praying together in a group, called the "teaspoon prayer". The only requirement is a teaspoon.

Question: What can this teaspoon teach us about prayer?

We use a teaspoon because of how it is often abbreviated, in recipe books to "tsp". This gives us the basic formula for prayer: Thanks, Sorry, Please. Any prayer using any of these elements is fine.

The essential part of praying together in a relaxed way is to start with telling each other what is on our minds - in our personal life, church life or national life. This means we do not need to turn prayers into a geography lesson, like, "Lord, we pray for our missionaries in Papua New Guinea, which, as you know Lord, is just north of Australia…"

After an introductory prayer, usually the Lord's Prayer, we pass the teaspoon round the group. Whoever has it can then pray a prayer aloud; if they do not want to, they simply pass the teaspoon on to the next person. It's a bit like the Native American pipe of peace. We end by saying the Grace.

GROUP PRAYER FOR OTHERS

1 We share what is on our hearts - personal, church, national, world-wide.

2 We pray the Lord's Prayer together.

3 We pass the teaspoon round the group, each person praying as he or she wishes while they hold it.

4 We end by saying the Grace together:
   May the grace of our Lord Jesus Christ,
   and the love of God,
   and the fellowship of the Holy Spirit
   be with us now and evermore. Amen.

FIVE STEPS TO FAITH

OTHER RESOURCES for Bible Ethics

A joke
God was sitting up on Mount Sinai when one day a tribe of nomads came and camped at the foot of the mountain. In the evening, God spoke to them out of the cloud. "Hey!" he called, "Do you want any commandments?" "What sort of commandments?" they replied. "Fairly general ones," God replied, "I am the only God, no idols, no work on the seventh day, that sort of thing." "Let us think about it," the nomads replied. But next morning, when God looked out, they'd gone.

A couple of month later, another group of nomads camped at the foot of Mount Sinai. In the evening, God called out, "Hey!" he called, "Do you want any commandments?" "What sort of commandments?" they replied. "The normal sort, " God replied, "Do not murder, do not commit adultery, do not steal." "We'll have to talk it over among ourselves," they replied, but in the morning they too had gone.

Several months later another group of nomads came to the mountain, led by a chap called Moses. In the evening, God called out. "Hey!" he called, "Do you want any commandments?" "How much are they," asked Moses."They're free!" said God. "All right," said Moses, we'll take ten."

Another joke
Around 1910 Alfred Marks' grandfather was highly respected in the Jewish community in the East End of London, and used to take part in a panel discussion in a cafe on Saturday evenings, after the sabbath. One day a young man asked if the panel could explain ethics. Alfred Marks' grandfather replied, "Ethics, ethics. A difficult subject. It's best if I give you a for instance. Me and my partner Max we run this haberdashery. One morning, while Max is out the back doing a stock take, a young lady comes into the shop and buys a very nice pair of kid gloves. She pays me £5. But, just as she is going out of the shop, I realise that by mistake she has given me two five pound notes stuck together. Now, here's where ethics comes in. Do, or do I not, tell my partner?"

The Ten Commandments expanded

The Ten Commandments are recorded in two places, in Exodus 20. 2-17 and in Deuteronomy 5.6-21. They are almost identical **except** for the reason given for keeping the Sabbath as a holy day. In Exodus it is because "in six days the LORD made heaven and earth…" (v.11). In Deuteronomy it is order to remember "that you were a slave in the land of Egypt, and the LORD brought you out from there…" (v.15) So it is clear that there has been some expansion of the text over time.

STEP 6 HANDOUT

Exodus 20.1 - (edited)

- I am the Lord your God, who brought you out of the land of Egypt, out of the house of slavery; you shall have no other gods before me.
- You shall not make for yourself an idol
- You shall not make wrongful use of the name of the Lord your God,
- Remember the sabbath day, and keep it holy.
- Honour your father and your mother.
- You shall not murder.
- You shall not commit adultery.
- You shall not steal.
- You shall not bear false witness against your neighbour.
- You shall not covet anything that belongs to your neighbour.

Isaiah 1.10-17

- Hear the word of the Lord,
  you rulers of Sodom!
  Listen to the teaching of our God,
  you people of Gomorrah!
  What to me is the multitude of your sacrifices?
  says the Lord;
  I have had enough of burnt-offerings of rams
  and the fat of fed beasts;
  I do not delight in the blood of bulls,
  or of lambs, or of goats.

- When you come to appear before me,
  who asked this from your hand?
  Trample my courts no more;
  bringing offerings is futile;
  incense is an abomination to me.
  New moon and sabbath and calling of convocation -
  I cannot endure solemn assemblies with iniquity.
  Your new moons and your appointed festivals
  my soul hates;

they have become a burden to me,
  I am weary of bearing them.
  When you stretch out your hands,
  I will hide my eyes from you;
  even though you make many prayers,
  I will not listen;
  your hands are full of blood.

- Wash yourselves; make yourselves clean;
  remove the evil of your doings
  from before my eyes;
  cease to do evil, learn to do good;
  seek justice, rescue the oppressed,
  defend the orphan, plead for the widow.

Romans 12.9-18, 21; 13.8-10

- Let love be genuine; hate what is evil, hold fast to what is good; love one another with mutual affection; outdo one another in showing honour. Do not lag in zeal, be ardent in spirit, serve the Lord. Rejoice in hope, be patient in suffering, persevere in prayer. Contribute to the needs of the saints; extend hospitality to strangers.

- Bless those who persecute you; bless and do not curse them. Rejoice with those who rejoice, weep with those who weep. Live in harmony with one another; do not be haughty, but associate with the lowly; do not claim to be wiser than you are. Do not repay anyone evil for evil, but take thought for what is noble in the sight of all. If it is possible, so far as it depends on you, live peaceably with all. Do not be overcome by evil, but overcome evil with good.

- Owe no one anything, except to love one another; for the one who loves another has fulfilled the law. The commandments, 'You shall not commit adultery; You shall not murder; You shall not steal; You shall not covet'; and any other commandment, are summed up in this word, 'Love your neighbour as yourself.' Love does no wrong to a neighbour; therefore, love is the fulfilling of the law.

FIVE STEPS TO FAITH

NOTES

Baptism
Decisions, decision, decisions: Starting the journey

WHAT PEOPLE THINK... about Baptism

From the Victoria and Albert Museum Tea Rooms:

"I always think of it as an insurance policy."

"I was baptised when I was 7 or 8, but it hasn't affected me significantly in my life."

"Like christening baptism? I think it's an interesting ritual."

"I think it's an interesting way of understanding forgiveness. I like the symbolic nature of it."

"A very important entry for young people into the church. It needs to be followed by confirmation."

"I actually don't think anything about it. I was baptised but my children weren't baptised."

FIVE STEPS TO FAITH

WHAT'S THIS STEP ABOUT?

This step explores what the Bible says about baptism, a Jewish ritual for Gentiles adopted by the Christian church. It can be an introduction to a baptism service in church, popularly known as christening when applied to babies.

LEARNING OUTCOMES

1 Decision Time
That baptism is about making a decision to live one's life under God.

2 The Holy Spirit
Baptism is linked to receiving the Holy Spirit (see Confirmation).

THE SESSION

FILM CLIP

We watch a short clip of "The Miracle Maker", just 2.5 minutes, from 7'30" to 10'. This covers the ministry of John the Baptist and the baptism of Jesus.

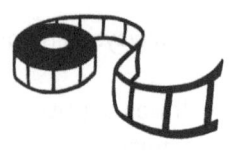

You could also watch the scene in "My Big Fat Greek Wedding" where Toula's fiancé is baptised in the local Greek Orthodox church: chapter 10 "Baptism", the first 3 minutes.

FIRST BIBLE BIT

Luke 3.3-22, edited
John the Baptist and the baptism of Jesus.

TEACHING POINT

Explain that "baptise" was an ordinary Greek word, most often used by sailors.

If possible, Take people to the kitchen and fill a bowl with water. Take a sponge and sprinkle some of the water over it. "Has this sponge been baptised?' 'No, it hasn't'. Get the sponge wetter and wetter until it is fully submerged. Then ask if it has been baptised. The answer, finally, is yes.

Explain that the word was used for shipwrecks. A good example of a baptised ship would be the Titanic. So the imagery of baptism is not cleansing, but death. Dying and coming up to a new life.

FIRST DISCUSSION

Key question: When the religious leaders came out to check up on John, he called them a "brood of vipers". (Matthew 3.7) Why?

I think it was because baptism was used as a common thing for Jews of that time to practice, but it was always a way of turning Gentiles, non-Jews, into Jews. By baptising Jews, John was effectively excommunicating the whole nation! No wonder the authorities disliked him. See Mark 12.29-32.

Question: What kind of lifestyle did John expect of those who had been baptised?

Question: Why do you think Jesus wanted to be baptised? General discussion - there is no one right answer!

Key question: What happened to Jesus when he was baptised? The discussion will, one hopes, lead to spotting that the Holy Spirit showed up.

SECOND BIBLE BIT

John 3.1-12 (edited)
Being born of water and spirit.

SECOND DISCUSSION

Key question: The phrase "born again" should properly read "born from above". What does this tell us about becoming a Christian?

PRAYER

A time of silence. The CCC says the following prayer of surrender - the key prayer of Alcoholics Anonymous (p. 63). He/she could say it line by line, allowing people either to repeat it quietly or silently after him/her.

> "God, I offer myself to Thee -
> to build with me and to do with me as Thou wilt.
> Relieve me of the bondage of self,
> that I may better do thy will.
> Take away my difficulties,
> that victory over them
> may bear witness to those I would help
> of Thy Power, Thy Love and thy Way of life.
> May I do Thy will always! Amen."

AND TO FOLLOW:
The natural follow-on from this session is to meet up again to go through the baptism service itself, either at home, or, particularly if children over the age of 4 are involved, in church.

OTHER RESOURCES on Baptism

Curious facts

1. The normal way of baptism in the Middle Ages was by "dipping", i.e. full immersion. The Book of Common Prayer (1552, 1558, 1662) describes the action as follows: *"the Priest shall take the Child into his hand, and shall say to the Godfathers and Godmothers, Name this child. And then after naming it after them (if they shall certify him that the Child may well endure it) he shall dip it in the Water discreetly and warily... But if they certify that the Child is weak, it shall suffice to pour Water upon it..."*

2. The orthodox church continues the original practice of anointing in olive oil the candidate for baptism - all over. It is a major job for the godparents. In the West oil, if used, I is simply used to put the sign of the cross on the candidate's forehead. But then we don't produce olive oil in Britain. They also submerge the person being baptised **three** times; in the name of the Father, the Son and the Holy Spirit.

FIVE STEPS TO FAITH

BAPTISM HANDOUT

Luke 3.2-22 (edited)

Narrator The word of God came to John son of Zechariah in the wilderness. He went into all the region around the Jordan, proclaiming a baptism of repentance for the forgiveness of sins, as it is written in the book of the words of the prophet Isaiah,
'The voice of one crying out in the wilderness:
"Prepare the way of the Lord,
make his paths straight.
Every valley shall be filled,
and every mountain and hill shall be made low,
and the crooked shall be made straight,
and the rough ways made smooth;
and all flesh shall see the salvation of God." '
John said to the (Pharisees and Sadducees*) that came out to be baptized by him,
John 'You brood of vipers! Who warned you to flee from the wrath to come? Bear fruits worthy of repentance. Do not begin to say to yourselves, "We have Abraham as our ancestor"; for I tell you, God is able from these stones to raise up children to Abraham. Even now the axe is lying at the root of the trees; every tree therefore that does not bear good fruit is cut down and thrown into the fire.'
Narrator And the crowds asked him, '
All What then should we do?'
John 'Whoever has two coats must share with anyone who has none; and whoever has food must do likewise.'
Narrator Even tax-collectors came to be baptized, and they asked him,
Tax collector 'Teacher, what should we do?'
John 'Collect no more than the amount prescribed for you.'
Narrator Soldiers also asked him,
Soldier 'And we, what should we do?'
John 'Do not extort money from anyone by threats or false accusation, and be satisfied with your wages.'

Narrator As the people were filled with expectation, and all were questioning in their hearts concerning John, whether he might be the Messiah, John answered all of them,

John 'I baptise you with water; but one who is more powerful than I is coming; I am not worthy to untie the thong of his sandals. He will baptise you with the Holy Spirit and fire. His winnowing-fork is in his hand, to clear his threshing-floor and to gather the wheat into his granary; but the chaff he will burn with unquenchable fire.'

Narrator With many other exhortations, he proclaimed the good news to the people.

Now when all the people were baptized, and when Jesus also had been baptized and was praying, the heaven was opened, and the Holy Spirit descended upon him in bodily form like a dove. And a voice came from heaven, 'You are my Son, the Beloved; with you I am well pleased.'

(* from the gospel of Matthew)

John 3.1-12 (edited)

Narrator Now there was a Pharisee named Nicodemus, a leader of the Jews. He came to Jesus by night and said to him,
Nicodemus 'Rabbi, we know that you are a teacher who has come from God; for no one can do these signs that you do apart from the presence of God.'
Jesus 'Very truly, I tell you, no one can see the kingdom of God without being born from above.'
Nicodemus 'How can anyone be born after having grown old? Can one enter a second time into the mother's womb and be born?'
Jesus 'Very truly, I tell you, no one can enter the kingdom of God without being born of water and Spirit. What is born of the flesh is flesh, and what is born of the Spirit is spirit. Do not be astonished that I said to you, "You must be born from above." The wind blows where it chooses, and you hear the sound of it, but you do not know where it comes from or where it goes. So it is with everyone who is born of the Spirit.'
Nicodemus 'How can these things be?'
Jesus 'Are you a teacher of Israel, and yet you do not understand these things? Very truly, I tell you, we speak of what we know and testify to what we have seen; yet you do not receive our testimony. If I have told you about earthly things and you do not believe, how can you believe if I tell you about heavenly things?'
Narrator No one has ascended into heaven except the one who descended from heaven, the Son of Man. And just as Moses lifted up the serpent in the wilderness, so must the Son of Man be lifted up, that whoever believes in him may have eternal life. For God so loved the world that he gave his only Son, so that everyone who believes in him may not perish but may have eternal life.

Note: Ancient Greek had no punctuation - indeed, no spaces between words. The inverted commas here are my guess of where Jesus' direct words to Nicodemus finish, though many Bibles put the whole passage into the mouth of Jesus.

NOTES

FIVE STEPS TO FAITH

Confirmation
A solution looking for a problem: Embracing the journey

WHAT PEOPLE THINK... **about Confirmation**

From HTB Queens Gate's, St Augustine's:

"Well, it's receiving the Holy Spirit, when you're 12 or 13. That's confirmation."

"Where to start? It's an opportunity to actively confirm a decision made on your behalf by your parents."

"I wasn't saved in this church and we don't have confirmation."

"Well, I'm confirmed. My parents kind of made me do it."
(a 17 year old)

'Oh, now, I was confirmed at school. We all dressed up in our white dresses. I don't know what to think about it honestly."

FIVE STEPS TO FAITH

WHAT'S THIS STEP ABOUT?

This session explores the history and practical use of Confirmation as, maybe, a sacrament.

We end with an experiment with *'lectio divina'* or Bible meditation on the Holy Spirit.

It can be part of the process of preparing for confirmation.

LEARNING OUTCOMES

1 Church history
That the church and the faith, as we experience it, is the result of two thousand years of church history. Things both change and remain the same.

2 The Holy Spirit
That the Holy Spirit makes all the difference to a Christian's life.

3 Prayer and meditation
That it is possible to hear the Holy Spirit speak to us through the Bible.

THE SESSION

There is no film at the start of this session. Instead, a short talk can be given, giving the historical background to confirmation. It is a complicated story, but I found that people rather appreciate hearing about the nuts and bolts of the church's development through the ages. Make as much or as little use of all this as you want.

HISTORICAL INTRODUCTION
1 The first three centuries

In the first three or four centuries, this is how you became a Christian:

a) You would be introduced to the bishop by an existing Christian who would vouch for you. The bishop would ask you various questions. For instance, if you were a soldier, you would be asked if you were ordered to kill someone, would you disobey the order. If your answer was 'no', you would be asked to come back when you had changed your mind. At least this was often the case in the Western church.

b) You would then undergo a course of instruction during Lent. That meant attending lectures every day of the 40 days of Lent, morning, afternoon and evening. If you lived outside the city you would need to find lodgings in the city.

c) On the evening of Easter night you would come to the church. On entering you would publicly renounce the devil. At midnight you would stand up and proclaim publicly why you wanted to be a Christian. You would then undress and have olive oil spread all over you like an athlete for Christ. You would then be plunged into the baptismal font - perhaps 4 metres across (like the one under Milan cathedral), put on new white clothing, and be given a new name. Then the bishop would lay his hands on your head and pray for you to receive the Holy Spirit. As dawn was breaking , you would receive the bread and wine of Holy Communion for the first time in your life.

In some churches you were not told what was going to happen, so the whole thing must have been a considerable shock to the system! And what your unbelieving husband thought of it could be a major problem.

FIVE STEPS TO FAITH

2   4th - 15th centuries

When Christianity became a state religion, the number of people wanting to become Christians grew exponentially. More churches sprang up in the cities, and it became impossible for the bishop of the city to baptise all the new converts. So the job was delegated. In the Western church, the local priests would baptise the converts in their own church on Easter Day, but the bishop would go round visiting all the churches in the city, laying his hands on each of the newly baptised persons for them to receive the Holy Spirit.

By this time all babies were baptised as soon as possible, and the bishop would confirm the baptised children when he next visited their church. That worked all right if your diocese was the size of Milan, but was a very different kettle of fish if your diocese was the size of Yorkshire. Bishops would try to visit each place roughly every seven years, and would then confirm everyone from the age of 7 down to infancy. There was a dispute in the 13th century in the English church whether confirmation should be given at the age of 1 or at the age of 3. But then the age of confirmation began being delayed to 7, or 10, or 13.

In the Eastern church, by contrast, baptism, confirmation and first communion were all carried out by the local priest at the same time. As infant baptism became the norm, the baby would be anointed with oil all over by a godparent, immersed completely in the water of the font or have a jugful of warm water poured over him/her, receive prayer for the Holy Spirit with the laying on of hands, and be given his/her first communion. This is done by having bread soaked in wine and being given in a teaspoon. Perhaps this is why a silver teaspoon was/is a traditional baptism gift.

3 a) The Reformation

In 1517 a German theological professor and monk, Martin Luther, published 95 challenges to what he perceived as abuses in the church. The papacy responded by unsuccessfully trying to quash this insubordination. Unsuccessful because of the new power of the printing press. By 1530 new Protestant churches were established in Germany and Switzerland and beyond. In 1549 this movement attained power in England, and after the brief reign of the catholic Queen Mary, a firmly Protestant church was established in 1558 under Elizabeth I.

This new church movement included a radical simplifying of theology, so that only two sacraments were considered genuine, baptism and holy communion. In 1562 the bishops and clergy in England set out their position in the 39 Articles of Religion:

Sacraments ordained of Christ be not only badges or tokens of Christian men's profession, but rather they be certain sure witnesses, and effectual means of grace, and God's good will towards us, by the which he doth work invisibly in us, and doth not only quicken, but also strengthen and confirm our Faith in him.

There are two Sacraments ordained of Christ our Lord in the Gospel, that is to say, Baptism, and the Supper of the Lord.

Those five commonly called Sacraments, that is to say, Confirmation, Penance, Orders, Matrimony, and extreme Unction, are not to be counted as Sacraments of the Gospel, being such as have grown partly of the corrupt following of the Apostles, partly are states of life allowed in the Scriptures; but yet have not like nature of Sacraments with baptism, and the Lord's Supper, for that they have not any visible sign or ceremony ordained by God.

In the Catechism (1559), sacraments are defined as: *"an outward and visible sign of an inward and spiritual grace..."*

So, if Confirmation is not a Sacrament, what is it? The answer of the Reformers was that it was a teaching tool to bring young children to an adult faith.

The Church hath thought good to order, that none hereafter be confirmed , but such as can say the Creed, the Lord's Prayer, and the Ten Commandments; and can also answer such questions, as in the short catechism are contained... (from The Order of Confirmation, or Laying On of Hands upon those who are baptized and come to the years of discretion, 1558)

Children were to be instructed in some part of the catechism on Sundays after the second lesson of Evening Prayer, which was traditionally held at 3.00. Only after the 1830s was there a movement to shift the time of Evening Prayer to 6.30; and the teaching of the Catechism to children during the service disappeared.

The Reformers were clear that an adult faith was important for everyone, and that confirmation was the sign. But there was also the ancient tradition that baptism was the entry point into the faith and in principle those who were baptised should be able to receive communion. So in the Book of Common Prayer it was laid down that *"there shall none be admitted to the holy Communion, until such time as he be confirmed,* **or be ready and desirous to be confirmed;"** (my emboldened letters), a loophole which bishops and parish clergy have largely ignored.

3 b) the Counter-Reformation

On the other hand, the Roman Catholic Church pronounced at the Seventh Session of the Council of Trent in 1547:

If anyone says that the confirmation of those baptized is a useless ceremony and not a true and proper sacrament; or that of old it was nothing more than a sort of catechesis (teaching) in which those nearing adolescence gave an account of their faith before the Church, let him be accursed.

However, the Roman Catholic Church has always insisted that it should be given to those who had reached the age of discretion, which was interpreted as the age of 7. If an adult, i.e. someone over the age of 14, was to be baptized, he/she should be confirmed immediately after.

3 c) the Methodist Church
The Methodist Church was the product of the amazing evangelisation to Britain carried out by John Wesley in the 18th century. Their worship is very similar to that of the Church of England, from which it arose, but its pattern of ministry is different, i.e. no bishops. So Confirmation is carried out by the local minister.

4   20th - 21st Centuries: The Problem of Communion
The situation changed on 30 June 1932. It was then that the Roman Catholic Church gave permission for Holy Communion to be given before confirmation. At first this was meant for exceptional circumstances but has now become the norm. So the traditional pattern of baptism, confirmation and communion is effectively baptism, communion, confirmation. The Church of England decided in 2006 to allow this to happen in some dioceses, provided that that each parish had its proposals for the teaching and support of children approved by the bishop. So a typical parish might baptise infants, usually at 6 months, give holy communion after preparation to children of about 7, and have young people confirmed from 11 years old and upwards.

At the same time the modern service books set down as the norm a threefold pattern of baptism, confirmation and communion all taking place in the same service. Increasingly confirmation is a step which adults take. In 2016 45% of confirmations which took place in the Church of England were of people who were 20 or over.

5   What's the point?
Theologically, confirmation is a bit of a mess. But in terms of people coming to faith and having the opportunity to receive a fresh touch of the Holy Spirit through prayer, it is invaluable. As a Church of England bishop, Stephen Cottrell, has said:

"Confirmation is the blossoming of baptismal life into active and whole-life discipleship… It is a sacramental ministry of grace, a fresh outpouring of the Holy Spirit. It makes faith fizz."

FIVE STEPS TO FAITH

FIRST BIBLE BIT

Acts 2.38, 8.5-8, 14-17
Peter's call to the crowd at Pentecost; then the mission to Samaria, when baptism and the laying on of hands were separated for the first time.

DISCUSSION

Key question: Do you think that baptism and confirmation should happen together or separately?

PRAYER & BIBLE MEDITATION

One way of hearing the Holy Spirit is to meditate on the Bible on one's own or in a small group. It was practised regularly in the monasteries for hundreds of years under the Latin term *'lectio divina'* or *'divine reading'*.

There are two principal ways. The older way is to read a Bible passage, and find a phrase which speaks to you, and then to spend some minutes reflecting quietly on it. The phrase in the traditional collect, or weekly prayer, about the holy Scriptures, is not a bad description. There we pray that we might *"read, mark, learn and inwardly digest them "*

The other way, started by Ignatius Loyola (1491-1556), the founder of the Jesuits, is to spend time entering imaginatively into a scene from the Gospel story and try to hear what Jesus might say to oneself in it.

The passage we are going to meditate on is one of the key passages about the Holy Spirit. John calls him "the Advocate" - a translation of the Greek and Latin word Paraclete. Essentially it means someone who stands by you.

John 14.15-20, 23, 25-6

We read it twice through as a group, perhaps with different people taking different paragraphs. Then we have 5 minutes' silence while we reflect on it. (N.B. It is important to specify the length of time of the silence, and to time it.)

At the end of 5 minutes, someone could read it again. Then, taking it in turn, each repeats one phrase or verse which has particularly spoken to them. **N.B This is not the time to giving voice to one's own opinions.** It is a time to hear what God has said to each of us through the scripture and in the silence. My experience is that every person focuses on a different verse, but if two or three repeat the same verse, that is absolutely OK.

When everyone has read their verse aloud, there can be a general discussion of what the passage means to us.

We end the session with the Lord's Prayer and the Grace.

CONFIRMATION HANDOUT

Acts 2.38
- On the day of Pentecost Peter said to them, 'Repent, and be baptized every one of you in the name of Jesus Christ so that your sins may be forgiven; and you will receive the gift of the Holy Spirit.

Acts 8.5-8, 14-17
- Philip went down to the city of Samaria and proclaimed the Messiah to them. The crowds with one accord listened eagerly to what was said by Philip, hearing and seeing the signs that he did, for unclean spirits, crying with loud shrieks, came out of many who were possessed; and many others who were paralysed or lame were cured. So there was great joy in that city.

- Now when the apostles at Jerusalem heard that Samaria had accepted the word of God, they sent Peter and John to them. The two went down and prayed for them that they might receive the Holy Spirit (for as yet the Spirit had not come upon any of them; they had only been baptized in the name of the Lord Jesus). Then Peter and John laid their hands on them, and they received the Holy Spirit.

John 14.15-20, 23, 26

- If you love me, you will keep my commandments. And I will ask the Father, and he will give you another Advocate, to be with you for ever. This is the Spirit of truth, whom the world cannot receive, because it neither sees him nor knows him. You know him, because he abides with you, and he will be in you.

- I will not leave you orphaned; I am coming to you. In a little while the world will no longer see me, but you will see me; because I live, you also will live. On that day you will know that I am in my Father, and you in me, and I in you.

- Those who love me will keep my word, and my Father will love them, and we will come to them and make our home with them.

- But the Advocate, the Holy Spirit, whom the Father will send in my name, will teach you everything, and remind you of all that I have said to you.

FIVE STEPS TO FAITH

NOTES

Holy Communion

or Eucharist, Mass, Divine Liturgy, Lord's Supper etc.

Bread for the journey

WHAT PEOPLE THINK... **about Communion**

From HTB Queens Gate's, St Augustine's:

"I think it's the ultimate. You're receiving the body and the blood. When I go to a service and receive communion, I feel full."

"I like it. It's something not enough places do, and people don't explain why we do it."

"Something I've been taught is very important, something we should take seriously and not light-heartedly."

"It's definitely not blood, it's definitely not a body. You don't have it every week, but it is important. It can become a ritual."

"OK. Umm. I think sharing a cup is a bit gross."

"It's the only thing that saves my whole existence. I don't think I could exist without it."

FIVE STEPS TO FAITH

WHAT'S THIS STEP ABOUT?

This step looks at the origin of holy communion in the last meal Jesus had before he was arrested and crucified. We go on to explore what communion might mean for us.

It can be part of the process of preparing for confirmation.

LEARNING OUTCOMES

1 What Jesus meant
To get an idea of what Jesus may have meant when he used those mysterious words, "This is my body, this is my blood of the covenant."

2 What we mean
To see that sharing in holy communion can link us to God.

THE SESSION

FILM CLIP

We watch a short clip of "The Miracle Maker", just 3.5 minutes, from 55' to 58'30". This shows the Last Supper Jesus which had with his disciples.

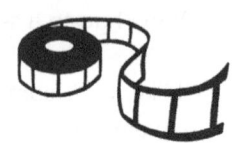

FIRST BIBLE BIT

Mark 14.12-26

FIRST DISCUSSION

Key questions: What might Jesus have meant when he said "This is my body" and "This is my blood"?
Where else in Jerusalem was there killing and blood?
What is a covenant?

SECOND BIBLE BIT

1 Corinthians 11.23-26 (written about 57 AD).

SECOND DISCUSSION

Key question: What does it mean "to remember the Lord's death till he comes"?

A READING
In 1552 Archbishop Cranmer wrote about his own understanding of Holy Communion in the Book of Common Prayer:

"As the benefit is great, if with a true penitent heart and lively faith we receive that holy Sacrament; (for then we spiritually eat the flesh of Christ, and drink his blood; then we dwell in Christ and he in us; we are one with Christ and he with us;) so is the danger great, if we receive the same unworthily..."

THIRD DISCUSSION

Key question: If we identify with Christ and he with us, how would this affect our lives?

PRAYER AND WORSHIP

In the Orthodox Church there is a tradition of "Blessed bread". In Western churches it is called "Agapé" from the word for "love" i.e. a love-feast. This is not consecrated bread as in Holy Communion, but bread as a sign of Christian fellowship. A key aspect is that we share the bread with somebody else. Here is a short service very much adapted from Orthodox Vespers which can be used as an "Agapé" service with which to end this session on Communion.

The service is fully set out in the handout.

COMMUNION HANDOUT

Mark 14.12-26

Narrator On the first day of Unleavened Bread, when the Passover lamb is sacrificed, his disciples said to him,
Disciple 'Where do you want us to go and make the preparations for you to eat the Passover?'
Narrator So he sent two of his disciples, saying to them,
Jesus 'Go into the city, and a man carrying a jar of water will meet you; follow him, and wherever he enters, say to the owner of the house, "The Teacher asks, Where is my guest room where I may eat the Passover with my disciples?" He will show you a large room upstairs, furnished and ready. Make preparations for us there.'
Narrator So the disciples set out and went to the city, and found everything as he had told them; and they prepared the Passover meal.

When it was evening, he came with the twelve. And when they had taken their places and were eating, Jesus said,
Jesus 'Truly I tell you, one of you will betray me, one who is eating with me.'
Narrator They began to be distressed and to say to him one after another,
All 'Surely, not I?'
Jesus 'It is one of the twelve, one who is dipping bread into the bowl with me. For the Son of Man goes as it is written of him, but woe to that one by whom the Son of Man is betrayed! It would have been better for that one not to have been born.'
Narrator While they were eating, he took a loaf of bread, and after blessing it he broke it, gave it to them, and said,
Jesus 'Take; this is my body.'
Narrator Then he took a cup, and after giving thanks he gave it to them, and all of them drank from it.
Jesus 'This is my blood of the covenant, which is poured out for many. Truly I tell you, I will never again drink of the fruit of the vine until that day when I drink it new in the kingdom of God.'
Narrator When they had sung a hymn, they went out to the Mount of Olives.

1 Corinthians 11.23-26

For I received from the Lord what I also handed on to you, that the Lord Jesus on the night when he was betrayed took a loaf of bread, and when he had given thanks, he broke it and said, 'This is my body that is for you. Do this in remembrance of me.' In the same way he took the cup also, after supper, saying, 'This cup is the new covenant in my blood. Do this, as often as you drink it, in remembrance of me.' For as often as you eat this bread and drink this cup, you proclaim the Lord's death until he comes.

BREAKING OF THE BREAD

Opening Prayer said by the person leading the session

O Lord Jesus Christ our God, Who did bless the five loaves and with them did feed the five thousand: May You, the same Lord, bless this loaf, and multiply it in this holy place, and in all the world; and sanctify all the faithful who shall share in it. For it is You, O Christ our God, Who blesses and sanctifies all things; and to You we ascribe glory: with the Father Who has no beginning, and Your all-holy, good, and life-creating Spirit, now and ever, and unto the ages of ages. **Amen.**

Psalm 34 (edited)
The leader starts. All say the words in bold

I will bless the Lord at all times;
his praise shall continually be in my mouth.
My soul makes its boast in the Lord;
let the humble hear and be glad.
O magnify the Lord with me,
and let us exalt his name together.

I sought the Lord, and he answered me,
and delivered me from all my fears.
Look to him, and be radiant;
so your faces shall never be ashamed.
This poor soul cried, and was heard by the Lord,
and was saved from every trouble.
The angel of the Lord encamps
around those who fear him, and delivers them.
O taste and see that the Lord is good;
happy are those who take refuge in him.

Come, O children, listen to me;
I will teach you the fear of the Lord.
Which of you desires life,
and covets many days to enjoy good?
Keep your tongue from evil,
and your lips from speaking deceit.
Depart from evil, and do good;
seek peace, and pursue it.

The eyes of the Lord are on the righteous,
and his ears are open to their cry.
The face of the Lord is against evildoers,
to cut off the remembrance of them from the earth.
When the righteous cry for help, the Lord hears,
and rescues them from all their troubles.
The Lord is near to the broken-hearted,
and saves the crushed in spirit.

Many are the afflictions of the righteous,
but the Lord rescues them from them all.
He keeps all their bones;
not one of them will be broken.
Evil brings death to the wicked,
and those who hate the righteous will be condemned.
The Lord redeems the life of his servants;
none of those who take refuge in him will be condemned.

Glory to the Father and to the Son and to the Holy Spirit,
As it was in the beginning, is now, and shall be for ever. Amen

Sharing the bread
The bread is distributed to everyone in the room, but not eaten until the gospel passage starts to be read. As someone reads John 6.35-40, we quietly share some bread with our neighbours and eat it ourselves. At the end of the reading, we keep silence.

Closing prayer
Lord Jesus, stay with us,
for the day is passing and the evening is at hand;
be our companion on the way,
kindle our hearts with love and joy,
and let us know you in your risen power,
for you are our Lord and God. **Amen.**

We can end by standing, holding hands if that is OK, and saying the Grace together:
>   **May the grace of our Lord Jesus Christ**
>   **and the love of God**
>   **and the fellowship of the Holy Spirit**
>   **be with us all**
>   **now and for evermore. Amen.**

OTHER RESOURCES

A Story
In the 1980's Father Bill Kirkpatrick, a priest in Ears Court, ministered to an enormous number of people dying of HIV/AIDS. He lived in a basement flat and had converted the coal cellar into a small chapel. He would celebrate Holy Communion there daily, whether or not he had any bread or wine in the flat, and with whoever was with him at the time. One morning he celebrated it with a cheese cracker and a glass of whiskey!

The Book of Common Prayer
The Book of Common Prayer was published in 1552, re-published in 1559, and re-re-published with minor changes in 1662. The key passage which expresses the theology of Holy Communion comes in the communion service, but is never read. That is because it comes in a series of three exhortations, printed in small print, in the middle of the service. These exhortations are:

1 Giving notice of when the next service of the holy Communion will be celebrated;
"He hath given his Son our Saviour Jesus Christ, not only to die for us. but also to be our spiritual food and sustenance in that holy Sacrament."

2 Declaring when the next service of holy Communion will be celebrated, but specially because people are "negligent" in coming to it;
"As the Son of God did vouchsafe to yield up his soul by death upon the Cross for your salvation; so it is your duty to receive the Communion, in the remembrance of the sacrifice of his death..."

3 A general Exhortation setting out the importance of holy Communion. This is the one the quote leading up to the third discussion is taken from. Further on in the exhortation comes this passage:
"And to the end that we should alway remember the exceeding great love of our master and only Saviour Jesus Christ, thus dying for us, and the innumerable benefits which by his precious blood-shedding he hath obtained to us; he hath instituted and ordained holy mysteries, as pledges of his love, and for a continual remembrance of his death, to our great and endless comfort."

What is a covenant?
In legal terms, a covenant is very different from a contract. A contract is an agreement between two parties. Each of them has responsibilities. A covenant is one-way. It is a free offer from one person to another which can create a relationship. It is easy to see why Christians and Jews talk about the relationship of God with his people as a covenant.

NOTES

Keep Calm and Carry on Learning

If people have met up for 5 or 6 weeks, that should not, one hopes, put a stop on their exploring and learning about the Christian faith. Here are a few suggestions amid the myriad books, films, and internet resources that are on offer.

THE CHRISTIAN FAITH

Questions of Life by Nicky Gumbel, the book which accompanies the Alpha course. Readable, informative, persuasive, written from an evangelical viewpoint.

Mere Christianity by C.S.Lewis. Written over 70 years ago, but still valuable. He starts from zero faith, which is bracing.

Basic Christianity by John Stott A sound, sensible guide to the Christian faith.

Encountering Light by Gonville ffrench-Beytagh He was Dean of Johannesburg South Africa and was deported because of his opposition to apartheid. A passionate man and a passionate book. Out of print, but available on Amazon.

THE BIBLE

Bible in Brief gives a structured overview of the Bible, 4 months Old Testament, 2 months New Testament. (I wrote it to replace a very useful little book, **Seeing the Bible Whole**, which is now out of print). Each month and each week has a separate topic, so you can choose what you want to read. Each passage has a question which you can respond to either in the book itself or on a discussion forum on line. Have a look at the website **bibleinbrief.org**. You may need to scroll down the home page to look inside the book.

Bible Reading Fellowship has four four-monthly booklets for daily reading which either look at particular books of the Bible or are more devotional.

Other daily reading schemes are available from Scripture Union, Crusade for World Revival, Our Daily Bread etc

There are websites for all the above, also **bibleinoneyear.org**, daily readings with commentary by Nicky and Pippa Gumbel.

PRAYER

When I Awake: thoughts on keeping the morning watch/ The Morning Quiet Time by Jack Winslow. Published in 1938 and still going strong. Really helpful in getting one praying. He spent many years in India and it shows in the depth of his spirituality. He was a strong supporter of the Oxford group, and chaplain at Lee Abbey, a Christian holiday centre in North Devon, for 14 years. Available on Amazon, just, and also from Lee Abbey, North Devon, at **relax@leeabbey.org.uk**.

Discovering Psalms as Prayer by me, Andy Roland . It faces all the problems of prayer and the psalms head on and with humour. I wrote it to share how one service in a Christian ashram in India became my inspiration for over 30 years. You can have a look at it, and buy it, at **bibleinbrief.org**.

School for Prayer/Beginning to Pray (the same book!) by Anthony Bloom, he was a Russian Orthodox bishop in London. Simple and inspiring.

SOME PRAYER WEBSITES

sacredspace.ie; Daily meditation with Irish Jesuits. Calming and encouraging;

churchofengland.org, Morning and Evening Prayer, Prayer during the Day, and Night Prayer.

Centre for Action and Contemplation/cac.org daily mediations from Richard Rohr OFM "How to incarnate love by unveiling the image and likeness of God in all that we see and do."

and many, many others!

NOTES

WHO HAS TAKEN PART

Date started	Name	Comments

An invitation to
www.bibleinbrief.org

On this website you can:

- Look inside all of Rev Andy's books and buy them online, p&p free.

- **Bible in Brief**
  Read an introduction to the book and the author.
  Access all the Bible readings for 6 months.
  Contribute your thoughts on any of the readings online.

- **Discovering Psalms as Prayer**
  Download all the prayer service sheets and listen to a few simple psalm chants.

- **The Book of Job**
  Access the suggested orchestral music for the musical interludes in order to put it on as a public performance.

- **A Week of Prayer in Jerusalem**
  Access all the photos in the book and more, full size.

- **Five Steps to Faith**
  Download all the handouts for the sessions on A4 format.

Plus...
- Watch nine brilliant half hour animated films on Old Testament characters. 'Moses' won the Primetime Emmy award for Outstanding Achievement in Animation.
- Read the Bible blog, with a new blog about various aspects of the Bible, posted every Thursday.
- Register and receive a monthly newsletter and update.

You can also contact Rev Andy on: facebook@revandybooks
twitter@rev_andy_books
linkedin/andrewroland

Lightning Source UK Ltd.
Milton Keynes UK
UKHW02f1917180418
321279UK00007B/158/P